Grade 3

Making Meaning®

SECOND EDITION

DEVELOPMENTAL STUDIES CENTER

Strategies That Build Comprehension and Community

Second edition published 2008.

Making Meaning is a registered trademark of Developmental Studies Center.

Developmental Studies Center wishes to thank the following authors, agents, and publishers for their permission to reprint materials included in this program. Many people went out of their way to help us secure these rights and we are very grateful for their support. Every effort has been made to trace the ownership of copyrighted material and to make full acknowledgment of its use. If errors or omissions have occurred, they will be corrected in subsequent editions, provided that notification is submitted in writing to the publisher.

"Feeling the Heat" by Kathryn R. Satterfield. Copyright © 2007 *TIME For Kids*. Reprinted by permission. "Why Do Animals Play?" reprinted by permission of Cricket Magazine Group, Carus Publishing Company, from *ASK Magazine* May/June 2007, Vol. 10, No. 5, text copyright © 2007 by Kathleen Weidner Zoehfeld. Excerpt from *Reptiles: A True Book* by Melissa Stewart, copyright © 2001 Children's Press, a Division of Grolier Publishing Co., Inc. All rights reserved.

All articles and texts reproduced in this manual and not referenced with a credit line above were created by Developmental Studies Center.

Developmental Studies Center
2000 Embarcadero, Suite 305
Oakland, CA 94606-5300
(800) 666-7270, fax: (510) 464-3670
devstu.org

ISBN: 978-1-59892-724-5

Printed in the United States of America

3 4 5 6 7 8 9 10 MLY 17 16 15 14 13 12

Table of Contents

Unit 5

Wondering/ Questioning

NARRATIVE NONFICTION (BIOGRAPHY)

During this unit, the students identify what they learn from a nonfiction text, use wondering/questioning and schema to make sense of nonfiction, and visualize as they listen to text. During IDR, the students use comprehension strategies to make sense of the texts they read independently and they continue to monitor whether they are making sense of what they read. Socially, they continue to take responsibility for their learning and behavior and they contribute ideas that are different from their partners' ideas.

Week 1 *Brave Harriet* by Marissa Moss

Week 2 *Wilma Unlimited* by Kathleen Krull

Week 1

Overview

UNIT 5: WONDERING/QUESTIONING
Narrative Nonfiction (Biography)

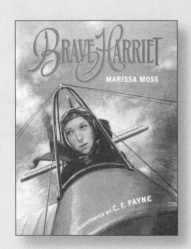

Brave Harriet
by Marissa Moss, illustrated by C. F. Payne
(Harcourt, 2001)

In aviation's early days, fearless Harriet Quimby makes history by becoming the first woman to fly solo across the English Channel.

ALTERNATIVE BOOKS

Kate Shelley and the Midnight Express by Margaret K. Wetterer

Cesar Chavez (Famous Americans) by Lola M. Schaefer

Comprehension Focus

- Students identify what they learn from a nonfiction text.

- Students use *wondering/questioning* to make sense of nonfiction.

- Students read independently.

Social Development Focus

- Students take responsibility for their learning and behavior.

- Students develop the group skill of contributing ideas that are different from their partners' ideas.

DO AHEAD

- Prior to Day 1, decide how you will randomly assign partners to work together during the unit.

- Title a sheet of chart paper "Brave Harriet" and divide the paper into two columns. Label the first column "What We Learned" and the second column "What We Wonder." (See Day 1, Step 4 on page 241.)

- Collect a variety of nonfiction texts for the students to read independently during this unit (see "About Nonfiction" on page 238).

- (Optional) Have a map of the western hemisphere ready to show the students.

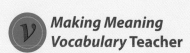

Making Meaning Vocabulary Teacher

If you are teaching Developmental Studies Center's *Making Meaning Vocabulary* program, teach Vocabulary Week 14 this week. For more information, see the *Making Meaning Vocabulary Teacher's Manual.*

Read-aloud/Strategy Lesson

In this lesson, the students:

- Identify what they learn from a nonfiction text
- *Wonder* about the text
- Read independently for up to 30 minutes
- Begin working with new partners
- Share their thinking

About Nonfiction

In this unit, the students will read nonfiction texts. Provide a variety of narrative nonfiction (especially biographies and autobiographies) and expository text for them to read independently. Expository texts include books, magazines (for example, *ASK, Discover, Ranger Rick,* and *Scholastic News*), and newspapers. For information about Developmental Studies Center's Individualized Daily Reading Libraries, see page xxvii and visit Developmental Studies Center's website at devstu.org.

▶ 1 Pair Students and Get Ready to Work Together

Randomly assign partners and have them sit together. Explain that for the next two weeks the students will work with their assigned partners.

Tell the students that during today's lesson they will hear part of a book and talk in pairs about it. You will ask them to report on their partner conversations at the end of the lesson. Ask:

Q *What did you do the last time you worked with a partner that will help you work with your new partner?*

Materials

- *Brave Harriet* (pages 4–17)
- "Brave Harriet" chart, prepared ahead (see Step 4)
- Map of the western hemisphere
- "Reading Comprehension Strategies" chart
- "IDR Conference Notes" record sheets

Being a Writer™ **Teacher**
You can either have the students work with their *Being a Writer* partner or assign them a different partner for the *Making Meaning* lessons.

Introduce *Brave Harriet* and Build Background Knowledge

Show the cover of *Brave Harriet* and read the title and the names of the author and illustrator aloud. Explain that *Brave Harriet* is a biography, and that a *biography* is a *true story about a real person*. Explain that this biography is about Harriet Quimby, who was the first American woman to receive a pilot's license. Harriet dreamed of being the first woman to fly across the English Channel. Use a map to locate Harriet's planned route across the English Channel, from Dover, England, to Calais, France.

Explain that *Brave Harriet* takes place about 100 years ago, when airplanes were a recent invention. Show the illustration on page 15 and discuss ways that airplanes of Harriet's day were different from today's airplanes. Point out that the planes had no radios, radar, or other methods of communicating with other planes or people on the ground.

Explain that today you will read the first part of the book aloud, and that you will stop during the reading to have partners share what they are learning about Harriet's life. At the end of the reading, you will record both information the students learned and questions they have about Harriet's life.

 Read *Brave Harriet* Aloud with Brief Section Introductions

Explain that the first part you will read describes how Harriet became a pilot. Ask the students to listen for how that happened. Start reading on page 5, showing the illustrations as you read.

> **Suggested Vocabulary**
>
> **gawky:** clumsy, awkward (p. 5)
>
> **longing:** strong wish (p. 5)
>
> **cutting figure eights:** flying in the shape of the number 8 (p. 6)
>
> **pylons:** towers (p. 6)
>
> **compass:** instrument that shows the direction in which one is traveling (p. 8)
>
> **fraud:** fake; person who claims to be what she is not (p. 10)
>
> **goggles:** protective glasses (p. 17)

 Note

Your English Language Learners will benefit from hearing the story and seeing the illustrations prior to today's read-aloud. In addition, you may want to take some time to explain the challenges that pilots faced 100 years ago.

◀ **Teacher Note**

This week's read-aloud contains a lot of factual information that the students might have difficulty following. To support them, you will briefly introduce each section before you read it. This will help to focus the students' listening on the main ideas discussed in that section.

ELL Vocabulary

English Language Learners may benefit from discussing additional vocabulary, including:

gum-and-spit contraption: (idiom) something held together badly, as if by gum and spit (p. 5)

soar: fly high above the ground (p. 5)

flew solo: flew a plane alone (p. 6)

could be the death of you: (idiom) could kill you (p. 8)

Stop after:

p. 6   "That's when I decided to do it—to become the first
         woman to fly solo across the English Channel."

Ask:

Teacher Note ▶

If the students do not offer
ideas beyond the background
knowledge you gave them during
the introduction, ask them what
else they learned about what
Harriet did to become a pilot.

You may wish to use a map
to clarify what Hamel means by
"…if you're off by a mere five
miles, you'll end up over the
North Sea." Point out that the
North Sea is very large and cold.

Q *What did you learn about how Harriet became a pilot?*

 Have the students use "Turn to Your Partner" to discuss the question. Then ask a few volunteers to share their ideas.

Explain that the next part of the book tells about Gustav Hamel, Harriet's good friend who was also a pilot. Ask the students to listen for what they learn about Harriet and Gustav. Reread the last sentence on page 6 and continue reading to the next stopping point:

p. 13   "Instead, he came with me to Dover to see me off."

Ask:

Q *What did you learn about Gustav and Harriet in this part of the story?*

 Have the students use "Turn to Your Partner" to discuss the question. Then have a few students share their ideas.

Reread the first paragraph on page 13, and continue reading to the end of the page. Pause and ask the students to think about whether Harriet has made the right decision. Then continue to read to the bottom of page 17. Stop after:

p. 17   "At 5:35 A.M. my plane left England's soil, heading over the
         cliffs of Dover, across the Channel, and on to France."

Ask:

Q *What did you learn in the part of the story you just heard?*

 Have the students use "Turn to Your Partner" to discuss the question.

▶4 Discuss What the Students Learned and What They Wonder

Tell the students that one reason people read biographies, or books about real people's lives, is to learn facts about them and their accomplishments. Have the students use "Turn to Your Partner" to discuss:

Q *If someone asked you what you learned about Harriet Quimby today, what would you answer? What are some important things you learned about her life?*

Direct the students' attention to the "Brave Harriet" chart. Have a few students share what they learned and record their ideas in the "What We Learned" column of the chart.

Remind the students that *wondering,* or *questioning,* is a strategy that can help them think about what they are reading. First in pairs, and then as a class, discuss:

Q *Based on what you know so far about Harriet Quimby, what do you wonder about her?*

Record two or three of the students' responses as "I wonder" statements or questions in the "What We Wonder" column of the chart.

> ***Students might say:***
>
> "I wonder if Harriet will really fly across the Channel."
>
> "I wonder if she will fly in the wrong direction and get lost. Gustav said she might."
>
> "Why couldn't many women be pilots then?"
>
> "I wonder if Harriet will get cold in the plane."

FACILITATION TIP

During this unit, we invite you to focus on **pacing** whole-class discussions so that they are lively and focused. A class discussion should be long enough to allow thinking and sharing, but short enough to sustain the attention of all the students. Good pacing during a discussion requires careful observation of all the students—not just those responding—and the timely use of pacing techniques such as:

- Use wait-time before calling on anyone to respond.

- Call on only a few students to respond to a question, even if others have their hands up.

- If many students want to respond, use "Turn to Your Partner" to give partners an opportunity to share with each other. Then call on two or three students to share with the whole class.

- If a discussion goes off topic, restate the question.

Explain that tomorrow you will read the rest of *Brave Harriet* and the students will learn more about her flight across the English Channel.

Save the "Brave Harriet" chart for Day 2.

5 Reflect on Working Together

 Have partners briefly discuss how their partner work went. Point out ways you noticed students contributing to their partner conversations and treating each other respectfully.

INDIVIDUALIZED DAILY READING

6 Document IDR Conferences/Review Reading Comprehension Strategies

Direct the students' attention to the "Reading Comprehension Strategies" chart and remind them that these are the strategies they have learned so far this year. Ask them to notice which strategies they use and where they use them during their reading today.

Have the students read books at their appropriate reading levels independently for up to 30 minutes.

Use the "IDR Conference Notes" record sheet to conduct and document individual conferences.

At the end of independent reading, have each student share his reading and a strategy he used—the name of the strategy and where he used it—with his partner. Students who cannot think of a comprehension strategy they used can talk about what they read.

As the students share, circulate among the pairs, listen, observe the students' behaviors and responses, and make notes. You might want to share some of your observations with the class.

If time permits, have a few students share their partner conversations with the class.

Reading Comprehension Strategies

- *making connections*

 ELL Note

When conferring with students with limited English proficiency, pay close attention to nonverbal evidence of comprehension, such as pointing to characters in story illustrations or acting out story events. During the conference, you may wish to provide the students with a chance to draw to demonstrate comprehension.

Day 2

Read-aloud/Strategy Lesson

In this lesson, the students:

- Identify what they learn from a nonfiction text
- *Wonder* about the text
- Read independently for up to 30 minutes
- Contribute ideas that are different from their partners' ideas

Materials

- *Brave Harriet* (pages 18–30)
- "Brave Harriet" chart from Day 1
- "Reading Comprehension Strategies" chart
- "IDR Conference Notes" record sheets

▶ 1 Introduce and Briefly Model Contributing Different Ideas

Have partners sit together. Review that this year they have learned several skills to help them work with a partner, such as explaining their thinking, listening carefully to each other, and using prompts to add to other people's ideas.

Explain that today the students will focus on a new skill: contributing ideas that are different from their partners' ideas. Point out that this skill is especially useful when reading nonfiction books with lots of information, like *Brave Harriet*. If each partner contributes different ideas, together they can remember more information from the book.

Choose a volunteer to act as your partner. Show the cover of *Brave Harriet* and ask your partner:

Q *What do you remember about Harriet Quimby from the first part of the book?*

Model attentive listening as your partner talks; then model contributing a different idea. (You might say, "You said you remember how Harriet's friend tried to persuade her not to fly across the Channel. I remember that when Harriet went to get her pilot's license, a man told her that no woman had ever gotten one before.")

Ask partners to briefly practice the skill by discussing what they remember about Harriet from the first part of the book. Remind the students that both partners should share their thinking.

Encourage the students to continue to practice this skill with their partners today.

 Review the "Brave Harriet" Chart

Briefly review the "What We Wonder" column of the "Brave Harriet" chart. Explain that today you will read the rest of the book, stopping several times to have the students discuss what they learn about Harriet Quimby. Ask them to listen carefully for answers to their questions and to be aware of any new questions that come to mind.

 Read *Brave Harriet* Aloud with Brief Section Introductions

Remind the students that at the end of the first day's reading Harriet was leaving England in her plane, hoping to reach France by flying across the English Channel.

 Explain that the next section you will read tells about Harriet's flight across the English Channel. Read page 18, pausing to have partners visualize and briefly describe the scene before showing the illustration.

Brave Harriet

What We Learned	What We Wonder

 Note

Consider reviewing the first part of the story with your English Language Learners prior to today's read-aloud.

Suggested Vocabulary

compass heading: direction (p. 22)

pitch: tilt (p. 22)

pancake onto the water: land flat on the water (p. 22)

hoisted me aloft: lifted me up (p. 28)

eclipsed: was more important than (p. 28)

ELL Vocabulary

English Language Learners may benefit from discussing additional vocabulary, including:

clouded up: became hard to see through because they were covered with mist (p. 20)

fog had crept into my bones: being in the fog made me feel cold and sleepy (p. 22)

in triumph: because of my success (p. 28)

Continue reading and stop after:

> **p. 24**   "And now, below the clouds, I could see the coast
> of France."

Ask:

Q   *What have you learned about Harriet's flight across the
English Channel?*

Have the students use "Turn to Your Partner" to discuss the question.
Remind them to share different ideas. Then ask a few volunteers to
share their ideas with the class. Ask:

Q   *What do you wonder?*

Have two or three students share what they are wondering; then
reread the last sentence on page 24 and continue reading to
page 28. Stop after:

> **p. 28**   "As I warmed my hands around the wide, thick steaming
> bowl, I could see the headlines already: AMERICAN WOMAN
> FLIES OVER THE CHANNEL!"

Without showing the illustration, ask:

Q   *How is Harriet feeling right now?*

Have the students use "Turn to Your Partner" to discuss the question;
then have a few students share their thinking with the class. Reread
the last sentence; then read to the end of page 28 and show the
illustration. Ask:

Q   *What has happened? What does this mean for Harriet?*

If necessary, briefly explain that the Titanic was a brand-new luxury
ship that hit an iceberg and sank on its way from England to the
United States, killing more than a thousand passengers.

Reread the last sentence on page 28 and continue reading to the
end of the book.

4 ▶ **Discuss What the Students Learned and What They Wonder**

Facilitate a whole-class discussion about what the students learned and what they wonder. Remind the students to continue to use the discussion prompts they learned earlier. Ask:

Q *What did you learn about Harriet Quimby from today's reading?*

As the students share, add their ideas to the "What We Learned" column of the "Brave Harriet" chart. Refer to the "What We Wonder" column and ask the following questions. Be prepared to reread parts of the text that support the students' thinking.

Q *What questions were discussed in today's reading? How were they discussed?*

Q *Based on what you heard today, what do you still wonder about Harriet?*

Have a few volunteers share their questions with the class and add them to the chart.

5 ▶ **Reflect on Contributing Different Ideas**

Briefly discuss how the students did contributing different ideas. Ask questions such as:

Q *How was contributing different ideas helpful to you and your partner?*

Students might say:

"Hearing my partner's ideas helped me remember other things I learned about Harriet."

"In addition to what [Henri] said, sharing different ideas helped me listen better to my partner."

"Sometimes I had to think for a minute before I could think of something different to say, because my partner said the idea that I was planning to talk about."

Tell the students that they will have more opportunities to practice contributing different ideas in the next lesson.

INDIVIDUALIZED DAILY READING

 Document IDR Conferences/Review Reading Comprehension Strategies

Direct the students' attention to the "Reading Comprehension Strategies" chart and remind them that these are the strategies they have learned so far this year. Ask them to notice which strategies they use and where they use them during their reading today.

Have the students read independently for up to 30 minutes.

Use the "IDR Conference Notes" record sheet to conduct and document individual conferences.

At the end of independent reading, have several students share their reading and the comprehension strategies they used—the names of the strategies and where they used them—with the class.

> Reading Comprehension
> Strategies
>
> - making connections

Day 3

Materials

- *Brave Harriet* (page 32)
- *Student Response Book* pages 23–25
- "Brave Harriet" chart
- *Assessment Resource Book*
- *Student Response Book,* IDR Journal section

Guided Strategy Practice

In this lesson, the students:

- Identify what they learn from a nonfiction text
- *Wonder* about the text
- Use a double-entry journal to record their thinking
- Read independently for up to 30 minutes
- Contribute ideas that are different from their partners' ideas

▶1 Discuss What the Students Learned from Harriet Quimby's Life

Review that the students heard and discussed *Brave Harriet,* a biography of pilot Harriet Quimby. Remind them that a biography is the story of a real person's life.

Explain that sometimes readers learn lessons from a person's biography that they can apply to their own lives. Briefly discuss:

Q *What did Harriet do that was brave?*

Q *What did you learn about the way Harriet lived her life that you might like to remember and use in your own life?*

Students might say:

"Harriet did something even though people said she couldn't. I want to be an astronaut, so maybe if people say I can't do it, I'll keep trying anyway."

"Maybe thinking about Harriet will help me do new things that I'm scared to do."

"Harriet didn't panic when she thought her plane was going down. I learned that it's good to not panic in an emergency, because then you can think of a plan."

Introduce the "Author's Note"

Show the students the "Author's Note" on page 32 of *Brave Harriet* and explain that the author included the note to give readers more information about Harriet Quimby. Explain that you will read the note aloud, and ask them to think about what they learn.

 ## Read Aloud

Read the "Author's Note" aloud.

Suggested Vocabulary

decade: ten years (p. 32)

aviator: pilot (p. 32)

promote commercial aviation: try to get ordinary people interested in traveling by plane (p. 32)

foresaw: predicted (p. 32)

coincided: happened at the same time (p. 32)

ambitious: having a strong wish to achieve something (p. 32)

ELL Vocabulary

English Language Learners may benefit from discussing additional vocabulary, including:

setting her sights: deciding (p. 32)

so convinced was he that the flight was beyond a woman's ability: he was very sure that a woman would not be able to fly across the Channel (p. 32)

died doing what she loved, soaring into the blue: died in an airplane crash (p. 32)

Reread the "Author's Note"

Ask the students to turn to *Student Response Book* pages 23–24. Point out that this is a copy of the "Author's Note" you read aloud. Explain that you will reread the note aloud, and ask the students to follow along as you read. Explain that you are rereading to give the students another opportunity to hear and think about the note.

Reread the "Author's Note" slowly and clearly.

5 ▶ Use a Double-entry Journal to Record Ideas

Have the students turn to *Student Response Book* page 25, "Double-entry Journal About Harriet Quimby." Tell them that they will use this page to record what they learned about Harriet Quimby from the "Author's Note" and what they wonder about her. Direct their attention to the "Brave Harriet" chart and point out that the chart is an example of a double-entry journal that they completed as a group.

 Explain that you would like partners to discuss what they learned from the "Author's Note" and what they still wonder about Harriet. After the partner discussion, they will write one thing they learned in the first column of the double-entry journal and one thing they wonder in the second column.

Brave Harriet

What We Learned	What We Wonder

> **CLASS COMPREHENSION ASSESSMENT**
>
> Circulate among the students as they work. Ask yourself:
>
> **Q** *Are the students able to state what they learned from the excerpt?*
>
> **Q** *Is what they learned an accurate reflection of what is in the excerpt?*
>
> **Q** *Are the students able to use information in the excerpt to wonder about Harriet Quimby?*
>
> Record your observations on page 18 of the *Assessment Resource Book.*

6 ▶ Discuss the "Author's Note" as a Class

Facilitate a whole-class discussion using the following questions:

Q *What did you learn about Harriet Quimby from the "Author's Note"?*

Q *What do you wonder about her?*

As volunteers respond, add a few of their ideas to the "Brave Harriet" chart.

 ELL Note

You might support your English Language Learners by providing these prompts for their responses: "I learned…" and "I wonder…."

Reflect on Contributing Different Ideas

Facilitate a brief class discussion about how the students did today bringing up ideas that were different from their partners'. Have a few students tell about their experiences as they used this skill.

INDIVIDUALIZED DAILY READING

 Read Independently/Write About Strategies They Used in Their IDR Journals

Have the students read independently for up to 30 minutes.

As the students read, circulate among them. Observe their reading behavior and engagement with the text. Ask individual students questions such as:

Q *What is your book about?*

Q *What made you decide to read this book?*

Q (Nonfiction book) *What do you already know about [planets]? How does knowing this information about [planets] help you understand this book?*

Q *If you get stuck, what do you do to help you understand?*

At the end of independent reading, have each student write about her reading and a strategy she used—the name of the strategy and where she used it. Students who cannot think of a strategy they used may write about their reading. Allow time for any student who has finished a book to record it in her "Reading Log."

EXTENSIONS

Visualize Scenes in *Brave Harriet*

Reread some descriptive passages from *Brave Harriet* aloud, for example, the first paragraph on page 5 and the single paragraph on page 18. Have the students close their eyes and visualize what is happening. After the reading, have volunteers describe their visualizations and say which words and phrases helped them picture the scene in their minds. Be prepared to reread from the text to help the students remember details.

Do Further Research About Harriet Quimby

Review the "What We Wonder" column of the "Brave Harriet" chart with the class and identify questions that are not answered in the book. Have the students think of ways they might find out more information about Harriet Quimby; then give interested students time to research the unanswered questions and report their findings to the class.

Day 4

Independent Strategy Practice

In this lesson, the students:

- Identify what they learn and what they *wonder* in nonfiction text read independently
- Use a double-entry journal to record their thinking
- Share their thinking

1 ▶ Review Learning and Wondering About *Brave Harriet*

Ask partners to sit together. Remind the students that this week they heard you read *Brave Harriet* and recorded what they learned and wondered about Harriet Quimby. Explain that today they will use a double-entry journal to record what they learn and wonder about in their independent reading. Then they will meet with their partners to share the ideas they recorded.

2 ▶ Introduce the Double-entry Journal

Have the students turn to *Student Response Book* page 26, "Double-entry Journal About _____." Explain that as they read independently today they will use this double-entry journal to record what they learn and wonder. Ask them each to write the title of the text they are reading on the blank line at the top of the page.

3 ▶ Read Independently and Use the Double-entry Journal

Explain that the students will read independently for 10 minutes, and that you would like them to think about what they learn as they read. After 10 minutes, they will stop and record what they learned in their double-entry journals.

Materials

- *Student Response Book* page 26
- Nonfiction texts at appropriate levels for independent reading
- Small self-stick note for each student

◀ **Teacher Note**

To help the students review the week, you might show them the illustrations from *Brave Harriet* or ask them to review the "Brave Harriet" chart or the double-entry journal on *Student Response Book* page 25.

 Note

Consider modeling this activity for your English Language Learners.

Make sure that the students have a variety of nonfiction texts at appropriate reading levels available to them. Ask them to use a self-stick note to mark the place they begin reading today.

After 10 minutes of independent reading, ask the students to record what they learned.

Teacher Note ▶

Remind the students that rereading is a strategy readers often use to help them understand and remember what they read. Explain that rereading can be especially useful with nonfiction texts, which are often filled with facts and other information that can be hard to understand or remember after a single reading.

When most students have finished recording what they learned, explain that they will reread, starting again at the self-stick note. As they reread, you would like them to notice what they wonder about their book's topic. After 10 minutes, they will stop and record what they wondered.

At the end of 10 minutes, ask the students to record what they wondered in the second column of their double-entry journals.

4 ▶ Discuss the Reading

Use "Turn to Your Partner" to have the students discuss what they learned and wondered about. Encourage them to ask each other questions when necessary to help them understand their partners' thinking.

Have several volunteers share with the class what they learned and wondered. Probe the students' thinking by asking questions such as:

Q *What is the subject of your book?*

Q *What did you learn from your reading today? Did anything you learned surprise you?*

Q *What did you wonder about? Was what you wondered about explained in the book? If so, how?*

Explain that in the coming weeks the students will read and think more about nonfiction books.

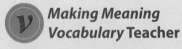

Making Meaning Vocabulary **Teacher**

Next week you will revisit *Brave Harriet* to teach Vocabulary Week 15.

Week 2

Overview

UNIT 5: WONDERING/QUESTIONING
Narrative Nonfiction (Biography)

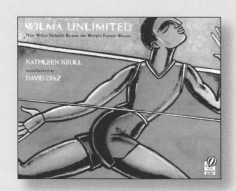

Wilma Unlimited
by Kathleen Krull, illustrated by David Diaz
(Voyager, 2000)

Wilma Rudolph overcomes polio to become a world-class runner and the first woman to win three gold medals in a single Olympics.

ALTERNATIVE BOOKS

Lou Gehrig: The Luckiest Man by David A. Adler

Satchmo's Blues by Alan Schroeder

Comprehension Focus

• Students identify what they learn from a nonfiction text.

• Students use *wondering/questioning* to make sense of nonfiction.

• Students read independently.

Social Development Focus

• Students take responsibility for their learning and behavior.

• Students develop the group skill of contributing ideas that are different from their partners'.

D O   A H E A D

• Title a sheet of chart paper "Wilma Unlimited" and divide the paper into two columns. Label the first column "What We Learned" and the second column "What We Wonder." (See Day 1, Step 4 on page 261.)

• Make copies of the Unit 5 Parent Letter (BLM19) to send home with the students on the last day of the unit.

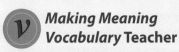

Making Meaning Vocabulary Teacher

If you are teaching Developmental Studies Center's *Making Meaning Vocabulary* program, teach Vocabulary Week 15 this week. For more information, see the *Making Meaning Vocabulary Teacher's Manual*.

Day 1

Materials

- *Wilma Unlimited* (pages 4–14)

- "Wilma Unlimited" chart, prepared ahead (see "Do Ahead," page 257)

- "Self-monitoring Questions" chart

- (Optional) A world map or globe

Read-aloud

In this lesson, the students:

- Identify what they learn from a nonfiction text
- *Wonder* about the text
- Read independently for up to 30 minutes
- Contribute ideas that are different from their partners' ideas

1 ▶ Review Contributing Different Ideas

Have partners sit together. Review that as they read *Brave Harriet* the students practiced contributing ideas different from their partners' ideas. Explain that this week they will continue to work on this skill. First in pairs, and then as a class, briefly discuss:

Q *How was contributing different ideas helpful to you and your partner when you talked about* Brave Harriet*?*

Remind the students to listen carefully to their partners today so that they can contribute different ideas to their partner conversations.

2 ▶ Introduce *Wilma Unlimited* and Build Background Knowledge

Show the cover of *Wilma Unlimited* and read the title and the names of the author and illustrator aloud. Explain that like *Brave Harriet,* this book is a biography. The book is about Wilma Rudolph, a woman who overcame many difficulties to become a champion runner.

Explain that Wilma, an African American, was born in Tennessee in 1940. She was one of many children, and her family did not have much money. Wilma's parents ▶ had to work hard to take care of their large family. At the time, black people in Tennessee and other states did not have the same rights as whites, and were often treated unfairly. For example, laws forced blacks to attend separate schools from whites. Blacks had to sit in the rear seats on public buses while whites sat up front. Explain that today it is against the law to treat people differently because of their race.

Teacher Note

During this discussion, you might point out Tennessee on a world map or globe. On Day 2, you can use the map or globe again to point out Rome, Italy, where the 1960 Summer Olympic Games took place.

3 ▶ Read *Wilma Unlimited* Aloud with Brief Section Introductions

Explain that today you will read the first part of *Wilma Unlimited* aloud, and that you will stop during the reading to have partners discuss the story. Direct the students' attention to the "Wilma Unlimited" chart, and point out that at the end of the reading you will record both information the students learn about Wilma and questions they have about her life.

Suggested Vocabulary

home remedies: medicines or treatments prepared at home from traditional practices (p. 4)

double pneumonia: disease of the lungs that makes breathing difficult (p. 6)

polio: disease that often leaves a person unable to walk (p. 8)

outhouse: outdoor toilet (p. 10)

paralyzed: not able to move (p. 10)

twitchy: moving with small jerky motions (p. 14)

ELL Vocabulary

English Language Learners may benefit from discussing additional vocabulary, including:

luxury: something expensive to use or buy (p. 6)

heaped: piled (p. 8)

permanently: forever (p. 8)

Explain that the first part you will read describes Wilma's family and her birth. Ask the students to listen to find out what she was like as a baby and what her family was like. Read page 4 twice. Stop after:

p. 4   "Most babies weren't Wilma Rudolph."

Ask:

Q   *What did you learn about baby Wilma and her family?*

Have the students use "Turn to Your Partner" to discuss the question. Then ask one or two volunteers to share their ideas with the class.

Explain that the next part you will read tells about hard times Wilma went through as a little girl. Ask the students to listen to find out what Wilma's early years were like. Reread the last sentence on page 4, and continue reading to the next stopping point:

> **p. 8**　"Wilma, that lively girl, would never walk again."

Ask:

Q　*What did you learn about Wilma in this part of the story?*

 Have the students use "Turn to Your Partner" to discuss the question. Then have a few students share their ideas. Ask:

Q　*What do you wonder?*

Have a few students tell the class what they are wondering about Wilma's life.

Explain that the next part you will read tells what Wilma's life was like after she came down with polio. Ask them to listen to find out what happened to Wilma after she got this serious illness. Reread the last paragraph on page 8, and continue reading to the next stopping point:

> **p. 14**　"Other times it just hurt."

Ask:

Q　*What did you learn about Wilma's life after she got polio?*

 Have the students use "Turn to Your Partner" to discuss the question.

 Discuss What the Students Learned and What They Wonder

Direct the students' attention to the "What We Learned" column of the "Wilma Unlimited" chart. Explain that first they will talk about what they learned about Wilma from today's reading. Remind them to contribute ideas that are different from their partners' ideas.

Ask:

Q *What are some important things you learned about Wilma's early life?*

First in pairs, and then as a class, have the students discuss the question. Then record a few of the students' ideas in the "What We Learned" column.

Next, refer to the "What We Wonder" column and ask:

Q *Based on what you know so far about Wilma Rudolph, what do you wonder about her?*

Have the students use "Turn to Your Partner" to discuss what they wonder. Then ask two or three volunteers to share their responses with the class. Record the responses as "I wonder" statements or questions in the second column of the chart.

Point out that, when possible, you will write a question in the "What We Wonder" column next to the "What We Learned" idea that triggered it. This shows that what they learn and what they wonder are related. For example, the chart might look like this:

Wilma Unlimited

What We Learned	What We Wonder
- Wilma had nineteen brothers and sisters.	
- Wilma was sick a lot.	- Why did she get so many diseases?
- Wilma's mom took care of her.	
- Wilma's leg was crippled from polio.	- How will Wilma become a good runner if she has polio?

Tell the students that tomorrow you will read more of *Wilma Unlimited* and the students will learn more about Wilma's life. Tomorrow's reading may answer some of their questions.

Save the "Wilma Unlimited" chart for Day 2.

▶5 Reflect on Working Together

Briefly discuss how partners worked together. Without identifying individuals, share examples you observed of partners contributing different ideas to their discussions.

INDIVIDUALIZED DAILY READING

▶6 Review and Practice Self-monitoring

Refer to the "Self-monitoring Questions" chart (see page 173) and review the questions on it. Remind the students of the importance of stopping to think about what they are reading and of using the questions to help them track when they are understanding their reading and when they are not. When they are not understanding, they may need to reread, use a comprehension strategy, or get a different book.

Have the students read books at their appropriate reading levels independently for up to 30 minutes. Stop them at 10-minute intervals and have them monitor their comprehension by thinking about the charted questions.

At the end of independent reading, have the students share their reading and how the self-monitoring questions helped them track their understanding.

Ask questions such as:

Q *Which question on the "Self-monitoring Questions" chart helped you the most in your reading today? Why?*

Q *If you decided to get a new book, why did you decide you needed to be reading a different book?*

Self-monitoring Questions

- What is happening in my story right now?

Note

You may wish to help your English Language Learners choose books at the right level by asking them to pick from a limited number of appropriate books that you have selected.

Day 2

Read-aloud

In this lesson, the students:

- Identify what they learn from a nonfiction text
- *Wonder* about the text
- Read independently for up to 30 minutes
- Contribute ideas that are different from their partners'

▶1 Review the "Wilma Unlimited" Chart

Refer to the "Wilma Unlimited" chart and briefly review the ideas listed there. Explain that today you will read more of *Wilma Unlimited*. Ask the students to listen carefully to see if their questions about Wilma are discussed in the reading. Also remind them to continue to practice contributing different ideas to their partner discussions.

▶2 Read Aloud with Brief Section Introductions

Remind the students that at the end of the first day's reading, Wilma was finally able to attend school. She was feeling sad because wearing a leg brace forced her to sit on the sidelines while other kids played games. Explain that the first section you will read today tells how Wilma continued to fight against her paralysis.

Suggested Vocabulary

faith: religious beliefs (p. 16)

triumphant: full of joy and pride (p. 20)

memorable: worth remembering; not easy to forget (p. 22)

full athletic scholarship: money given to an athlete to pay college expenses (p. 26)

Materials

- *Wilma Unlimited* (pages 16–38)
- "Wilma Unlimited" chart from Day 1
- "IDR Conference Notes" record sheets

<table>
<tr><td colspan="2" align="center">Wilma Unlimited</td></tr>
<tr><td>What We Learned</td><td>What We Wonder</td></tr>
</table>

ELL Vocabulary

English Language Learners may benefit from discussing additional vocabulary, including:

concentrating on: thinking hard about (p. 16)

propel her: move her quickly (p. 24)

Olympic Games: sports competition held every four years for athletes from around the world (p. 28)

The crowd went wild: The crowd shouted and clapped in excitement (p. 32)

Begin reading on page 16, and stop after:

> **p. 22** "As soon as Wilma sent that box away, she knew her life was beginning all over again."

Ask:

Q *What has happened to make Wilma think her life is beginning all over again?*

 Have the students use "Turn to Your Partner" to discuss the question; then have one or two volunteers share with the class. Ask:

Q *What do you wonder?*

Have two or three students share what they are wondering. Explain that the next part of the story describes how Wilma's life changed after she stopped wearing a leg brace. Reread the last sentence on page 22 and continue reading to the next stopping point:

> **p. 26** "She was the first member of her family to go to college."

Ask:

Q *What has happened to Wilma?*

 Have the students use "Turn to Your Partner" to discuss the question; then have one or two students share with the class. Explain that in the next part Wilma competes in the Olympic Games in Rome, Italy. Reread the last sentence on page 26 and continue reading to the next stopping point:

> **p. 28** "It was still swollen and painful on the day of her first race."

Ask:

Q *What do you wonder?*

Have a few students share what they are wondering about the story; then reread the last two sentences on page 28 and continue reading to the next stopping point:

> **p. 30** "An Olympic gold medal was hers to take home."

Explain that instead of reading pages 31–37 you will show the illustrations and paraphrase that part of the story. (For example, you might say, "Wilma is famous after she wins the 100-meter dash. She goes on to win the 200-meter dash, and now she has two gold medals. The last event Wilma competes in is a relay race. As her teammate passes her the baton, she stumbles and two competing runners pass her. But Wilma runs as fast as she can and wins the race for the United States—and her third gold medal.")

After paraphrasing pages 31–37, read the final page (page 38) aloud.

◀ **Teacher Note**

If necessary, use the illustration on pages 34–35 to explain that in a relay race each teammate runs a portion of the race and then passes a stick called a baton to the next runner on the team.

3▶ Discuss the Story

Facilitate a whole-class discussion about what the students learned and what they wondered in *Wilma Unlimited.* Ask:

Q *What did you learn about Wilma Rudolph in today's reading?*

Have a few students share what they learned and add the students' ideas to the "What We Learned" column of the "Wilma Unlimited" chart. Direct the students' attention to the "What We Wonder" column, and ask:

Q *What questions were discussed in today's reading? How were they discussed?*

Q *Based on what you heard today, what else do you wonder about Wilma?*

Have a few volunteers share their thinking with the class and add any new questions to the chart.

Explain that you will read from the "Author's Note" of *Wilma Unlimited* tomorrow.

4 ▸ Reflect on Taking Responsibility

Ask and briefly discuss:

Q *How did you take responsibility for your own learning today?*

Q *What is one thing you might do differently the next time you work with your partner to take more responsibility for your learning?*

INDIVIDUALIZED DAILY READING

5 ▸ Document IDR Conferences/Discuss What the Students Learned and What They Wonder

Tell the students that today you would like them to be aware of what they are learning and wondering as they read their books.

Have the students read independently for up to 30 minutes.

Use the "IDR Conference Notes" record sheet to conduct and document individual conferences.

At the end of independent reading, have one or two students who have not finished their books share with the class what they are learning and what they are wondering about their reading. Ask each student to read the title of his book to the class and briefly explain what the book is about and what he has learned from the book. Then have the student share with the class what he is wondering about the book.

ELL Note

Prior to IDR, tell your English Language Learners that you may ask them to share with the class what they have learned from reading their books, and what they are wondering. After IDR, support the students who share by providing them with prompts such as: "The title of my book is…," "It is about…," "I learned…," and "I wonder…."

Day 3

Guided Strategy Practice

In this lesson, the students:

- Identify what they learn from a text
- *Wonder* about the text
- Use a double-entry journal to record their thinking
- Read independently for up to 30 minutes
- Share their thinking

Materials

- *Wilma Unlimited*
- *Student Response Book* pages 27–28
- "Wilma Unlimited" chart
- *Student Response Book,* IDR Journal section
- "IDR Conference Notes" record sheets

1 **Discuss What the Students Learned from Wilma Rudolph's Life**

Review that the students heard two biographies, one of Harriet Quimby (*Brave Harriet*) and one of Wilma Rudolph (*Wilma Unlimited*). Remind the students that readers can often learn lessons from the life of the person in a biography that they can apply to their own lives. Ask:

Q *What was Wilma Rudolph like? What did she do that showed what she was like?*

Q *What did you learn about the way Wilma lived her life that you might like to remember and use in your own life?*

Students might say:

"Wilma kept on trying even though she had polio and her family was poor, so maybe if I think of her I'll keep trying when something is hard for me."

"In addition to what [Traci] said, Wilma was the fastest woman in the world. I'd like to be the first woman to do something like that."

2 ▶ Introduce the "Author's Note"

Show the students the "Author's Note" on page 40 of *Wilma Unlimited* and remind them that authors of biographies and other nonfiction books sometimes include notes that give additional information about the subject. Explain that this note tells what happened to Wilma Rudolph after she won her gold medals. Tell them that you will read parts of the note aloud and ask them to think about what they learn.

3 ▶ Read the "Author's Note" Aloud

Read the sections of the "Author's Note" that are reproduced on *Student Response Book* page 27 aloud.

Suggested Vocabulary

inspired: given hope to (p. 40)

ELL Vocabulary

English Language Learners may benefit from discussing additional vocabulary, including:

banquet: dinner for many people (p. 40)
dreaded: feared (p. 40)
celebrity: famous person (p. 40)

4 ▶ Reread the "Author's Note"

Teacher Note ▶

You may want to remind the students that the reason you are rereading the note is to give them another opportunity to hear and think about the information in it.

Ask the students to turn to *Student Response Book* page 27, and point out that this is a copy of the "Author's Note" sections you read aloud. Explain that you would like the students to follow along as you reread it.

Reread the *Student Response Book* page, slowly and clearly.

5 Use a Double-entry Journal to Record Ideas

Have the students turn to *Student Response Book* page 28, "Double-entry Journal About Wilma Rudolph." Explain that they will use the double-entry journal in their *Student Response Books* to record what they learned about Wilma Rudolph from the "Author's Note" and what they still wonder about her. Have partners talk about what they learned and wonder about Wilma. Then have each student write one or more things she learned in the first column of the double-entry journal and one or more things she still wonders in the second column. If the students wonder about something they learned, ask them to write these two items next to each other on the chart.

6 Share as a Whole Class

Facilitate a whole-class discussion about what the students learned and wonder. Ask:

Q *What did you learn about Wilma Rudolph from the "Author's Note"?*

Q *What do you still wonder about Wilma?*

Refer to the "Wilma Unlimited" chart and ask:

Q *What are some things we wondered about that are answered in the "Author's Note"?*

Q *What are some things we wondered about that haven't been answered?*

Explain that sometimes readers have questions that are not answered in a text. In these cases, readers can look in other texts to find answers to their questions. If the students are interested in Wilma Rudolph, suggest that they look for more information about her life in other books or on the Internet.

◄ Teacher Note

Circulate as the students work and notice whether they are identifying and recording what they learned and wonder about Wilma Rudolph. Have the students explain their thinking by reading supporting parts of the "Author's Note" to you. Help students who are struggling by reading the text along with them. This may be especially helpful for English Language Learners.

Wilma Unlimited

What We Learned	What We Wonder

INDIVIDUALIZED DAILY READING

 Document IDR Conferences/Have the Students Write About What They Learned and Wondered

Have the students read independently for up to 30 minutes.

Use the "IDR Conference Notes" record sheet to conduct and document individual conferences.

At the end of independent reading, have the students write about what they learned and what they wondered in their IDR Journals. If time permits, have a few students share what they learned and wondered with the class.

EXTENSION

Read About Other Olympic Athletes

Like Wilma Rudolph, many athletes have overcome formidable obstacles to become Olympic champions. Read about some other athletes (for example, *A Picture Book of Jesse Owens* by David A. Adler), and encourage the students to think about what they learn and what they wonder as they hear the book. After the reading, facilitate a class discussion about how these athletes' lives are similar to Wilma Rudolph's.

Teacher Note

This is the last week in which the "IDR Conference Notes" record sheets will appear in the Materials list; however, you should continue to use these sheets during IDR conferences for the rest of the year.

Day 4

Independent Strategy Practice

In this lesson, the students:

- Identify what they learn and *wonder* about in a nonfiction text read independently
- Use a double-entry journal to record their thinking
- Contribute ideas that are different from their partners' ideas

Materials

- *Student Response Book* page 29
- Nonfiction texts at appropriate levels for independent reading
- *Assessment Resource Book*
- Unit 5 Parent Letter (BLM19)

1 Review the Week

Review that this week the students heard *Wilma Unlimited* and used a double-entry journal to record what they learned and wondered about Wilma Rudolph. Explain that today they will use a double-entry journal to record what they learn and wonder about as they read independently.

Remind the students to continue to contribute ideas that are different from their partners' ideas during partner discussions.

2 Introduce the Double-entry Journal

Have the students turn to *Student Response Book* page 29, "Double-entry Journal About _____." Explain that as they read independently today they will use this double-entry journal to record what they learn and wonder. Ask them to each write the title of the text they are reading on the blank line at the top of the page.

 ELL Note

You may want to model this activity for your English Language Learners.

3 ▶ **Read Independently and Write in the Double-entry Journal**

Explain that the students will read independently for 10 minutes, and that you would like them to think about what they are learning as they read. After 10 minutes, they will record what they learned in the "What I Learned" column of the journal. Based on what they learned, they will write what they wonder about in the "What I Wonder" column.

Make sure the students have a variety of nonfiction texts at appropriate reading levels available to them. Have them read independently for 10 minutes.

After 10 minutes, have the students use the double-entry journal to record their ideas.

CLASS COMPREHENSION ASSESSMENT

Circulate as the students read. Ask yourself:

Q *Are the students able to identify what they are learning from their reading?*

Q *Are they able to wonder and ask questions about the reading?*

Record your observations on page 19 of the *Assessment Resource Book*.

4 ▶ **Discuss the Reading**

 Have the students use "Turn to Your Partner" to discuss what they learned and wondered about as they read. Ask each student to begin by telling his partner what the subject of the book is and what he read about today.

ELL Note

Whenever possible, it is beneficial to provide English Language Learners with books in their primary language.

FACILITATION TIP

Reflect on your experience over the past two weeks with **pacing** class discussions. Do the pacing techniques feel comfortable and natural? Do you find yourself using them throughout the school day? What effect has your focus on pacing had on the students' participation in discussions? We encourage you to continue to focus on pacing class discussions during the remainder of the school year.

Have a few volunteers share what they learned and wondered with the class. Probe their thinking by asking questions such as:

Q *What did you learn from your reading?*

Q *What did you wonder about? Was what you wondered about talked about in the book? If so, how?*

Reflect on the Students' Work Together

Review that the students focused this week on contributing different ideas from their partners'. Use "Think, Pair, Share" to have the students discuss:

Q *What did you do this week that helped you and your partner work well together? What did your partner do?*

Q *How did you take responsibility for your own learning this week?*

Teacher Note

This is the last week in Unit 5. You will reassign partners for Unit 6.

INDIVIDUAL COMPREHENSION ASSESSMENT

Before continuing with Unit 6, take this opportunity to assess individual students' progress in using *wondering/questioning* to make sense of their reading. Please refer to pages 36–37 in the *Assessment Resource Book* for instructions.

SOCIAL SKILLS ASSESSMENT

Take this opportunity to assess your students' social development using the "Social Skills Assessment" record sheet on pages 2–3 of the *Assessment Resource Book*. This assessment will occur again after Unit 7.

EXTENSION

Read More Biographies

Remind the students that during the past two weeks they heard and discussed two biographies. Use "Think, Pair, Share" to have the students think about and discuss other famous people they would like to read about. As a class, compile a list of people the students are interested in, and have the students find and read biographies about those people.

Parent Letter

Send home with each student the Parent Letter for this unit (see "Do Ahead," page 257). Periodically, have a few students share with the class what they are reading at home.

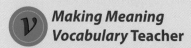

***Making Meaning Vocabulary* Teacher**

Next week you will revisit *Wilma Unlimited* to teach Vocabulary Week 16.

Unit 6

Analyzing Text Features

EXPOSITORY NONFICTION

During this unit, the students begin to explore text features in books, articles, and functional texts to help them make sense of expository texts. During IDR, they read expository texts independently. Socially, they continue to develop the group skill of contributing ideas that are different from their partners' ideas and continue to take responsibility for their learning and behavior.

Week 1 *Morning Meals Around the World*
by Maryellen Gregoire

Week 2 *Reptiles* by Melissa Stewart

Week 3 "Hop to It: Fancy Footwork"
"Origami: The Art of Japanese Paper Folding"
"How to Make a Paper Airplane"
"Lincoln School Lunch Calendar for
the week of May 21–25"

UNIT 6: ANALYZING TEXT FEATURES

Expository Nonfiction

Morning Meals Around the World
by Maryellen Gregoire, illustrated by Jeff Yesh
(Picture Window Books, 2004)

This book tells about the breakfast foods that people eat in different parts of the world.

ALTERNATIVE BOOKS

Food by Margaret C. Hall

Evening Meals Around the World by Michelle Zurakowski

Comprehension Focus

- Students *explore text features* in expository texts.

- Students identify what they learn from a text.

- Students read independently.

Social Development Focus

- Students take responsibility for their learning and behavior.

- Students contribute ideas that are different from their partners' ideas.

- Students participate in a class meeting.

DO AHEAD

- Prior to Day 1, decide how you will randomly assign partners to work together during the unit.

- Collect examples of expository texts from the classroom to show to the students on Day 1, Step 2.

- Prepare a chart with the title "Expository Text Features" (see Day 1, Step 3 on page 279).

- Collect a variety of expository texts for the students to examine and read independently on Day 3. (For information about expository texts, see "About Expository Text" on page 278. For information about Developmental Studies Center's Individualized Reading Libraries, see page xxvii and visit Developmental Studies Center's website at devstu.org.)

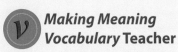

v **Making Meaning** *Vocabulary* **Teacher**

If you are teaching Developmental Studies Center's *Making Meaning Vocabulary* program, teach Vocabulary Week 16 this week. For more information, see the *Making Meaning Vocabulary Teacher's Manual.*

Read-aloud

Materials

- *Morning Meals Around the World*
- Examples of expository texts
- "Expository Text Features" chart, prepared ahead, and a marker
- *Student Response Book* pages 30–31

In this lesson, the students:

- Begin working with new partners
- *Explore text features* in expository texts
- Identify what they learn from a text
- Read independently for up to 30 minutes
- Contribute ideas that are different from their partners' ideas

About Expository Text

Nonfiction plays an increasingly important role in students' learning as they progress through the elementary grades. The students must be able to read and understand both narrative nonfiction—such as biographies, memoirs, and other true stories—and expository texts that are not written as stories. Expository texts include textbooks; newspapers; encyclopedias; Internet documents; functional texts such as directions, charts, and graphs; and many other informational texts.

During the next three weeks, the students will read expository texts and examine various text features. Collect enough examples of expository texts so that each student has at least one to examine. Use textbooks and trade books that contain a range of nonfiction text features including tables of contents, indexes, appendices, headings and subheadings, photos, maps, graphs, diagrams, framed text, and bold, italic, and colored type.

Also have available expository texts at various reading levels for independent reading.

Being a Writer™ **Teacher**
You can either have the students work with their *Being a Writer* partner or assign them a different partner for the *Making Meaning* lessons.

 ## Pair Students and Get Ready to Work Together

Randomly assign partners and have them sit together. Remind the students that they have been contributing ideas different from their partners' during their partner conversations. Tell them that they will continue to practice this skill this week.

Explain that you will check in during the week to see how their partner work is going.

Introduce Expository Text

Remind the students that in previous lessons they heard biographies of Harriet Quimby and Wilma Rudolph. Tell them that this week they will hear and read another type of nonfiction book called *expository text*. Explain that expository texts give readers information, just as biographies do, but they are usually organized around a specific topic, such as a type of animal or a place in the world, rather than organized as a story. Show the students examples of expository texts from your classroom library.

Introduce *Morning Meals Around the World* and Start the "Expository Text Features" Chart

Explain that expository books often look different from books that tell stories. They often include features that help the reader locate information in the text and understand the topic better. Explain that for the next several weeks the students will read expository texts, learn new information, and explore text features.

Show the cover of *Morning Meals Around the World* and read the title and the author's name aloud. Then show and read aloud the information on the back cover of the book. Explain that an expository nonfiction book often includes a summary on the back cover to let readers know what the book is about. Encourage the students to get in the habit of reading the back cover when they choose a book to read.

Tell the students that this week they will be exploring the text features in *Morning Meals Around the World* and you will list the text features they notice on the "Expository Text Features" chart. Direct the students' attention to the "Expository Text Features" chart, and write *summary on the back of the book*.

Explore the Table of Contents and Read Aloud

Show the students pages 4–5 of *Morning Meals Around the World* and explain that this feature, which is called the table of contents, tells readers what kind of information they will find in the book, as well as the page number where a chapter or section begins. Add *table of contents* to the "Expository Text Features" chart.

ELL Note

English Language Learners will benefit from previewing the text and the illustrations prior to the lesson.

◀ **Teacher Note**

If necessary, define *morning meals* as *breakfast* or *food eaten in the morning*.

Expository
Text Features

- summary on the back
  of the book

Have the students open their *Student Response Books* to pages 30–31 and have them look at the table of contents. Point out that this table of contents is organized on a world map; most tables of contents are organized in a list at the front of the book. Ask and briefly discuss:

Q *What do you notice about this table of contents?*

In pairs, have the students look at the table of contents and chose a country that they would like to learn about. After a minute, ask:

Q *Which country's morning meal do you want to find out about? On which page or pages in the book will we find that information?*

Choose one of the countries the students suggest and read that section aloud to the students. Repeat this process with several countries requested by the students. Deal with each suggested vocabulary word briefly as you encounter it in the text.

Suggested Vocabulary

zing: exciting flavor (p. 9)

tortilla: very thin round bread (p. 14; refer to the illustration)

veggies: vegetables (p. 17)

tofu: food made from soybeans (p. 18)

refreshing: cold and energizing (p. 22)

ELL Vocabulary

English Language Learners may benefit from discussing additional vocabulary, including:

travel: go (p. 4)

sugarcoated: covered with sugar (p. 6)

waffles: crisp cakes (p. 7; refer to the illustration)

pancake: flat thin cake (p. 8; refer to the illustration)

hot chocolate: warm drink flavored by chocolate (p. 10)

a popular way: liked by lots of people (p. 12)

rooster: male chicken (p. 17)

5 ▶ Discuss the Reading

Facilitate a whole-class discussion using the following questions. As the students respond, be ready to reread passages aloud and show illustrations again to help them recall what they heard. Ask:

Q *According to the book, what are some of the different meals people eat in the morning?*

Q *Which of the morning meals would you like to try? Why?*

Q *What surprised you about the different morning meals?*

Q *What do you eat for your morning meal?*

Remind the students that readers will often use the table of contents to find sections or chapters that contain information they want to learn more about. Encourage the students to use the table of contents to help them find information in expository texts.

Explain that tomorrow the students will continue to explore expository text.

INDIVIDUALIZED DAILY READING

6 ▶ Read Independently

Remind the students that thinking about what they already know about a topic can help them understand what they read about that topic. Ask the students to think about what they already know about the topics of their books before and during reading today.

Have the students read expository books independently for up to 30 minutes.

As the students read, circulate and ask individual students questions such as those on the next page.

FACILITATION TIP

During this unit, we encourage you to **avoid repeating or paraphrasing** students' responses. Repeating what students say when they speak too softly or paraphrasing them when they don't speak clearly teaches the students to listen to you but not to one another. Help the students learn to take responsibility by asking one another to speak up or by asking a question if they don't understand what a classmate has said.

Q *What did you already know about [whales]?*

Q *What have you learned about [whales] from your reading today?*

Q *Based on what you already know or what you are learning, what are you wondering about [whales]?*

 At the end of independent reading, have partners tell one another what they have learned.

EXTENSION

Draw and Write About Favorite Morning Meals

Give the students an opportunity to think about their favorite morning meals and discuss them in pairs. First in pairs, and then as a class, have the students discuss questions such as:

Q *What is your favorite morning meal?*

Q *What ingredients are used in the meal?*

Q *Who makes your favorite meal?*

Q *What do you like most about the meal?*

Have the students draw pictures and write about their favorite morning meals. Collect the students' papers and put them together into a class book of "Favorite Morning Meals."

Day 2

Strategy Lesson

In this lesson, the students:

- *Explore text features* in expository texts
- Identify what they learn from a text
- Read independently for up to 30 minutes
- Contribute ideas that are different than their partners' ideas

1 ▶ Review *Morning Meals Around the World* and Introduce the Index

Have partners sit together. Show the cover of *Morning Meals Around the World* and review that the students looked at the table of contents and heard about different morning meals from around world. Explain that today they will explore several text features often found at the end of expository nonfiction books and learn more about morning meals around the world.

Show the index on page 24 and explain that many nonfiction books have an index. Explain that readers can use an index to help them find specific information about topics mentioned in the book. Explain that an index is a list of words related to the subject of a book. The numbers listed beside the words in an index tell the reader where the words can be found in the text.

Have the students turn to *Student Response Book* page 32, and explain that this is a copy of the index from *Morning Meals Around the World*. Have the students follow along as you read the index aloud. If necessary, clarify any vocabulary as you read by simply stating which words are foods and which are countries. Have the students use "Think, Pair, Share" to discuss:

Q   *What do you notice about the index?*

Have a few volunteers share their thinking.

Materials

- *Morning Meals Around the World*
- *Student Response Book* page 32
- "Expository Text Features" chart and a marker
- "Reading Comprehension Strategies" chart and a marker

ELL Note

Provide extra support for your English Language Learners by previewing the index prior to today's lesson. Model for your students how to use the index.

Students might say:

"The words are in alphabetical order."

"Some words have one page number and some have more than one."

"It has some of the words from the parts we read yesterday.'"

Teacher Note ▶

If the students have difficulty answering the question, offer some suggestions like those in the "Students might say" note.

2 Explore the Index in Pairs and as a Class

Tell the students that partners will look at the index in their *Student Response Books* and together circle one or two words listed in the index that they want to learn more about.

Give the students a few moments to look over the index; then have a few pairs share the words they circled and explain why they are interested in those topics. Model using the index by turning to a page listed with the word a student suggests. Locate the word on the page and read aloud the sentence containing the word and, if appropriate, the entire paragraph in which the word is located. If the index indicates that a word can be found on more than one page, turn to that page next and follow the same procedure.

Teacher Note ▶

The words in the index are defined in the text and will be defined for the students as you read the passages that contain the words.

Tell the students that the index in a nonfiction book helps readers quickly find all the places in the book where a topic or a word is mentioned. Explain that readers often use the index if they have a question about a topic or want to find out more about it. Add *index* to the "Expository Text Features" chart.

3 Briefly Explore Other Text Features and Discuss Information from the Reading

Show the students page 24 of *Morning Meals Around the World* and explain that this page contains other text features sometimes found at the end of expository nonfiction books.

Point out the "Fun Facts" section and explain that this section gives extra information about morning meals from around the world.

Read the "Fun Facts" to the students and ask:

 Q *What did you learn about morning meals from the "Fun Facts" section?*

 ELL Note

You might prompt your English Language Learners to begin their response by saying, "I learned…."

Q *What fact did you think was fun? Why?*

Add *Fun Facts* to the "Expository Text Features" chart.

Draw the students' attention to the "To Learn More" section. Explain that this is a list of other books that are about different foods people eat around the world. This section is for readers who still have questions or want to find more information on the topic. Add *To Learn More* to the "Expository Text Features" chart.

Point to the glossary, and explain that a glossary is a list of words the author thinks readers might need to know to understand the book. Point out that it is organized like a dictionary; it lists the words in alphabetical order and tells what each word means. Add *glossary* to the chart.

 First in pairs, and then as a class, discuss the following question:

Q *What new information did you learn by exploring the text features of* Morning Meals Around the World?

4 ▶ Add to the "Reading Comprehension Strategies" Chart

Direct the students' attention to the "Reading Comprehension Strategies" chart. Review that the chart lists comprehension strategies they should be practicing when they read independently.

Remind the students that expository text features such as the table of contents, the index, and pictures with captions can help them learn more about the topic they are reading about. Add *recognizing text features* to the chart, and encourage the students to continue to look for more features and to think about how those features help them understand what they are reading.

5 ▶ Briefly Discuss Sharing Different Ideas

Review that the students have been working on contributing different ideas from their partners' ideas when they are talking in pairs. Briefly discuss the questions on the next page.

> *Reading Comprehension*
> *Strategies*
>
> *- making connections*

Q *How did contributing different ideas from your partner's add to your partner discussion?*

Q *What is one thing you want to do differently the next time you work with your partner? How will doing that help you and your partner work together?*

INDIVIDUALIZED DAILY READING

6 ▶ Read Independently

Have the students read expository books for up to 30 minutes. Ask the students to think about what they already know about the topics of their books before and during their reading today.

 At the end of independent reading, have partners tell each other what they have learned.

Day 3

Independent Strategy Practice

In this lesson, the students:

- Read independently
- Identify what they learn from expository text
- Identify features of expository text
- Contribute ideas that are different than their partners' ideas

1 Review Expository Text Features with *Morning Meals Around the World*

Have partners sit together. Show *Morning Meals Around the World* and review that the book is an example of an expository text— text that gives information about a topic. Remind the students that readers read expository texts to learn information about different subjects.

Ask and briefly discuss:

Q *What did you learn from* Morning Meals Around the World?

Briefly review the "Expository Text Features" chart, and discuss:

Q *How did looking at text features such as the table of contents and index help you understand more about what people around the world eat in the morning?*

Explain that today they will read their own nonfiction books and notice what they are learning both from the text and the text features.

2 Read Independently and Reread for Information

Make sure the students have a variety of expository texts at appropriate reading levels available to them. Ask them to use self-stick notes to mark the place they begin reading today and have

Materials

- *Morning Meals Around the World*
- "Expository Text Features" chart and a marker
- A variety of expository texts that students can examine and read independently
- Small self-stick notes for each student
- *Assessment Resource Book*

ELL Note

Consider modeling this activity for your English Language Learners.

them read independently. Stop the students after 10–15 minutes. Ask them to go back to the place they started reading, reread the text, and use additional self-stick notes to mark places in their texts where they learned something.

Circulate among the students as they read. If a student is struggling, support the student by asking questions such as:

Q *What are you reading about?*

Q *What have you learned about [Abraham Lincoln] from what you have read so far?*

 After another 10–15 minutes, stop the students. First in pairs, and then as a class, discuss the following questions:

Q *What did you learn from the book you read today?*

Q *Did your book have a table of contents and index? If so, how did they help you understand the text?*

Save the "Expository Text Features" chart for Week 2, Day 1.

CLASS COMPREHENSION ASSESSMENT

Circulate among the students as they work. Notice whether they understand the information they are learning from their texts.

Ask yourself:

Q *Do the students know what their books are about?*

Q *Are the students able to identify what they are learning in their texts?*

Record your observations on page 20 of the *Assessment Resource Book.*

Reflect on the Students' Work Together

Facilitate a brief discussion about how the students worked together. Ask:

Q *What did you do today that helped you and your partner work well together? What did your partner do?*

EXTENSION

List Expository Texts from Daily Life

Have the students use their IDR Journals to make an ongoing list of expository texts they read both in and outside of school. During the next two weeks, give the students regular opportunities to update their lists and share them with one another. Sharing the lists will help the students recognize how many kinds of expository texts they encounter and discover some of the reasons they read them. It will also make them aware of what their classmates are reading.

Day 4

Materials

- Space for the class to sit in a circle
- "Class Meeting Ground Rules" chart
- *Student Response Book,* IDR Journal section

Class Meeting Ground Rules

- one person talks at a time
- listen to one another

Teacher Note

Remind the students to use the discussion prompts they have learned, namely:

- *I agree with _____, because...*
- *I disagree with _____, because...*
- *In addition to what _____ said, I think...*

Class Meeting

In this lesson, the students:

- Review the ground rules and procedure for a class meeting
- Analyze the ways they have been interacting
- Share their thinking
- Read independently for up to 30 minutes

 1 **Have a Check-in Class Meeting**

Have the students move into a circle for a class meeting and review the class meeting ground rules.

Remind the students that they have been building a safe and supportive reading community this year. Explain that having a safe and supportive classroom community allows the students to share their thinking and agree and disagree comfortably with each other. Explain that the purpose of today's meeting is to discuss how they are contributing to the reading community and if they need to do anything different to help create a sense of community in the classroom. Ask the students to think about how they have interacted with their partners and other classmates in the past few weeks. First in pairs, and then as a class, discuss:

Q *What have you done to take responsibility for your own behavior and learning?*

Q *What can you do in the coming days to make sure you are being responsible?*

Students might say:

"I took responsibility by asking my partner and classmates
questions when I didn't understand something they said."

"In addition to what [Lupe] said, I asked people to repeat what
they said if I couldn't hear them."

"My partner contributed different ideas to our discussions
and that helped me learn more about what we were talking
about. I think he was taking responsibility when he brought up
new ideas."

"I'm going to work on listening more closely to what my partner
says and then contribute new ideas to our conversation."

As the students share, facilitate the conversation by asking
questions such as:

Q *[Lupe] said [she] took responsibility for [her] learning when
[she asked her partner questions]. Why is that a responsible
thing to do?*

Q *Why is it important to contribute your thinking to your
partner conversations? How does that help us build a
supportive reading community?*

Q *What can we do to be sure we [ask our classmates questions
when we don't understand] in the coming weeks?*

2 ▶ Reflect on the Class Meeting

Ask the students to analyze how they did today following the class
meeting ground rules. Ask questions such as:

Q *What do you think we need to continue to work on? Why?*

Q *What can you do to add to the next class meeting? How is that
taking responsibility?*

Remind the students to look for opportunities in the coming
weeks to take responsibility for their own behavior. Then, adjourn
the meeting.

INDIVIDUALIZED DAILY READING

 Document IDR Conferences/Have the Students Write About What They Learned

Have the students read independently for up to 30 minutes. Ask the students to pay attention to what information they are learning from their books. Explain that at the end of IDR the students will write about what they learned today in their IDR Journals.

Use the "IDR Conference Notes" record sheet to conduct and document individual conferences.

At the end of independent reading, have the students write about what they learned today from their expository books. Ask and briefly discuss:

Q *What information did you learn today about [outer space]?*

Q *How might you write about that information in your journal?*

As a class, briefly discuss the information the students wrote about.

 Note

If the students are struggling to write, have them draw or act out what they learned.

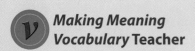 *Making Meaning Vocabulary* **Teacher**

Next week you will revisit *Morning Meals Around the World* to teach Vocabulary Week 17.

Week 2

Overview

UNIT 6: ANALYZING TEXT FEATURES

Expository Nonfiction

Reptiles
by Melissa Stewart
(Children's Press, 2001)

This book describes the basic behavior, physical characteristics, and life cycles of reptiles.

ALTERNATIVE BOOKS

Crocodiles by Sandra Markle

The Statue of Liberty by Patricia Ryon Quiri

Comprehension Focus

• Students *explore text features* in expository texts.

• Students identify what they learn from a text.

• Students *visualize* as they listen to text.

• Students *use schema* to make sense of nonfiction.

• Students read independently.

Social Development Focus

• Students take responsibility for their learning and behavior.

• Students contribute ideas that are different from their partners' ideas.

DO AHEAD

• Make a transparency of the "Contents from *Reptiles*" (BLM24) for Day 3.

• Collect a variety of expository texts for the students to examine and read independently on Day 3.

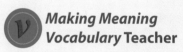

Making Meaning Vocabulary Teacher

If you are teaching Developmental Studies Center's *Making Meaning Vocabulary* program, teach Vocabulary Week 17 this week. For more information, see the *Making Meaning Vocabulary Teacher's Manual.*

Day 1

Materials

- *Reptiles* (pages 5–9)
- "Expository Text Features" chart from Week 1 and a marker

Read-aloud

In this lesson, the students:

- *Explore text features* in expository texts
- Identify what they learn from a text
- Read independently for up to 30 minutes
- Contribute ideas that are different from their partners' ideas

1 ▶ Get Ready to Work Together

Have partners sit together. Remind the students that during partner discussions they have been working on contributing ideas that are different from their partners' ideas. Ask and briefly discuss:

Q *How does contributing different ideas to your partner discussions help you and your partner learn more about the topic you are discussing?*

Ask the students to continue to add new ideas to their partner discussions today.

2 ▶ Introduce *Reptiles* and Add to the "Expository Text Features" Chart

Remind the students that in the previous lesson they heard the expository text *Morning Meals Around the World*. Tell them that this week they will hear and read another expository text. Remind them that expository texts give information about a topic and often include text features that provide additional information.

Explain that the expository text you will read today gives information about reptiles. Show the cover of *Reptiles* and read the title and the author's name aloud. Open the book to the copyright page, and point out the photo. Explain that in expository texts, photographs often come with a caption, or words that tell what the

 Note

ELL

Preview *Reptiles* with your English Language Learners prior to today's read-aloud.

photo shows. Explain that they will find photographs and captions in most expository texts.

Direct the students' attention to the "Expository Text Features" chart, and write *photographs* and *captions*.

Next, show the students the "Contents" page and explain that this table of contents looks different from the table of contents in *Morning Meals Around the World*. Remind the students that the *table of contents* tells readers what kind of information they will find in the book, as well as the page number where each chapter begins.

Explain that text features like photos with captions and tables of contents are included in expository texts to help readers make sense of the information in the book. Encourage the students to look for other features as you read aloud from *Reptiles* today.

 3 **Read Chapter 1 of *Reptiles* Aloud**

Explain that you will read Chapter 1, "What Is a Reptile?" aloud twice. The first time you will read without stopping; then you will reread, stopping to have partners talk about what they learned.

Suggested Vocabulary

basks: lies or sits (p. 5)

scales: small hard plates that cover the body of a reptile (p. 6)

moist: a little wet (p. 6)

cold blooded: having a body temperature that changes as air or water temperature changes (p. 8)

ELL Vocabulary

English Language Learners may benefit from discussing additional vocabulary, including:

mighty: strong (p. 5)

look like smaller versions of their parents: look like their parents but they are small (p. 6)

Read pages 5–9 aloud once without stopping or showing the photographs.

Expository
Text Features

- summary on the back of the book

◀ **Teacher Note**

Reading the text twice models for the students the importance of rereading to increase comprehension. You might want to point this out to the students.

Teacher Note

This lesson suggests not sharing with the whole class after each stop because this builds the students' independence and emphasizes the importance of partner discussion. However, if you notice that partners are having difficulty talking, you might have a few pairs report what they talked about after the first or second stop to provide discussion ideas for the other students.

Reread pages 5–9 aloud, stopping as described below. Show the photographs and read the accompanying captions. Stop after:

p. 7   "A turtle's scales cover a hard, bony shell."

 Have the students use "Think, Pair, Share" to discuss what they have learned about reptiles so far. After a few minutes, reread the last three sentences, and continue to read to the next stopping point:

p. 9   "By noon, a reptile may start to get too hot. To cool down, it hides in a shady place."

 Have the students use "Think, Pair, Share" to discuss what new information they have learned about reptiles.

FACILITATION TIP

This week continue to **avoid repeating or paraphrasing** the students' responses. Help them to learn to participate responsibly in class discussions by asking one another to speak up or by asking a question if they don't understand what a classmate has said.

4 ▶ Discuss the Reading

Facilitate a whole-class discussion using the following questions. As the students respond, be ready to show the photographs and reread the captions and passages to help them recall what they heard.

Q   *What did you learn about reptiles from the reading?*

Q   *What did you learn about reptiles from the photographs and captions?*

Explain that the students will hear more about reptiles in the next lesson.

INDIVIDUALIZED DAILY READING

5 ▶ Document IDR Conferences/Have the Students Discuss Text Features

Have the students independently read expository texts at their appropriate reading levels for up to 30 minutes. Ask the students to pay particular attention to the text features and to be ready to discuss those features with their partners at the end of IDR.

Use the "IDR Conference Notes" record sheet to conduct and document individual conferences.

At the end of independent reading, have the students discuss in pairs what they learned and any text features they noticed. As a class, discuss the different text features in the students' books.

EXTENSION

Add to the List of Expository Texts from Daily Life

Have the students add to their lists in their IDR Journals of expository texts they read both in and outside of school.

Day 2

Materials

- *Reptiles* (pages 38–39 and 46)
- *Student Response Book* pages 33–34
- "Expository Text Features" chart and a marker

Expository
Text Features

- summary on the back
  of the book

 Note

You might need to show the photographs to your English Language Learners to help them understand the reading.

Guided Strategy Practice

In this lesson, the students:

- *Visualize* to understand a text
- Identify what they learn from a text
- Read independently for up to 30 minutes
- Contribute ideas that are different from their partners' ideas

1 Introduce "Tales of Tuataras" and Add to the "Expository Text Features" Chart

Have partners sit together. Show the cover of *Reptiles* and remind the students that in the previous lesson they listened to and discussed the first chapter, "What Is a Reptile?" Refer to the "Expository Text Features" chart and review that they also learned about some features that help readers understand expository texts.

Explain that today you will read another part of *Reptiles* called "Tales of Tuataras," which tells about a reptile called the tuatara. Open *Reptiles* to page 46 ("Important Words"), and read the definition of tuatara: "a lizard-like reptile that lives on a few small islands near New Zealand." Explain that New Zealand is a large island-nation in the Pacific Ocean.

Show the "Important Words" page, and explain that a list of important words is the same as a glossary. Refer to the "Expository Text Features" chart and add *important words* next to *glossary*.

2 Read Aloud and Visualize

Explain that you will read "Tales of Tuataras" twice, but that you will not show the photographs. Explain that you would like the students to listen carefully to the description of the tuatara and visualize what the reptile might look like. Later they will draw a picture of what they visualized.

Read pages 38–39 aloud slowly and clearly, without stopping or showing the photographs.

Suggested Vocabulary

burrows: holes dug by animals for shelter (p. 39)
geckos: kind of lizard (p. 39)

ELL Vocabulary

English Language Learners may benefit from discussing additional vocabulary, including:

They cannot have young: They cannot have babies (p. 39)

3 ▶ Reread and Visualize

Have the students turn to page 33 in their *Student Response Books* and point out that this excerpt is the part of the book you just read aloud. Tell the students that you will read the passage again so they will have another opportunity to think about and visualize the tuatara. Explain that you would like the students to follow along in their *Student Response Books* as you reread the excerpt.

Reread the excerpt aloud. Ask, and briefly discuss:

Q *Using the description in the text, how do you visualize a tuatara?*

Ask the students to quickly sketch a tuatara on *Student Response Book* page 34. At the bottom of the page, have them write one thing they learned about tuataras.

4 ▶ Discuss the Reading and Drawings

Facilitate a brief discussion about what the students learned about tuataras. First in pairs, and then as a class, discuss the following questions. Remind the students to listen carefully to their partners and contribute different ideas from their partners' to the discussion.

Q *What are some things you learned about tuataras?*

Q *How did you visualize the tuatara? What words in the text helped you picture it?*

Q *What other things might you want to know about tuataras?*

Show the photographs on pages 38–39 and read the accompanying captions.

Explain that in the next lesson the students will learn more about expository texts and their special features.

INDIVIDUALIZED DAILY READING

5▶ Use Schema to Help Understand Nonfiction Text/ Read Independently

Remind the students that thinking about what they already know about a topic can help them understand what they read about that topic. Ask the students to think about what they already know about the topics of their books and then turn to their partners and share their thinking.

Have the students read expository books independently for up to 30 minutes.

At the end of independent reading, have the students tell their partners what they have learned and what they would like to learn more about.

ELL Note

Before your English Language Learners read independently, tell them that at the end of independent reading you will ask them to tell their partners what they learned from their reading and what they would like to learn more about.

Day 3

Guided Strategy Practice

In this lesson, the students:

- *Wonder* about a nonfiction text
- Identify features of expository text
- Think about how text features add to the meaning of expository text
- Read independently for up to 30 minutes
- Share their thinking

1 Review Expository Text and Wonder About *Reptiles*

Have partners sit together. Hold up *Reptiles* and review that the book is an example of expository text—text that gives information about a topic. Remind the students that they heard parts of the book and learned about reptiles and about a particular kind of reptile called the tuatara. Have the students use "Think, Pair, Share" to discuss:

Q *What are some things you wonder or want to know about reptiles?*

Have a few volunteers share their thinking with the class. Explain that you will not read the rest of the book aloud, but that you will make *Reptiles* available during IDR so interested students can read for answers to their questions.

2 Review Features and Explore the Contents Page

Refer to the "Expository Text Features" chart and review that expository texts often contain features that help readers make sense of the texts. Explain that today the students will look more closely at some features of the book *Reptiles,* beginning with the "Contents" page.

Materials

- *Reptiles* (pages 3 and 44–48)
- "Expository Text Features" chart and a marker
- "Contents from *Reptiles*" transparency (BLM24)
- A variety of expository texts that students can examine and read independently
- *Student Response Book* page 35
- *Assessment Resource Book*
- *Student Response Book,* IDR Journal section

◀ **Teacher Note**

If necessary, stimulate the students' thinking by leafing through *Reptiles*, reading chapter titles, and showing photographs. You might also suggest some ideas of your own (for example, "I want to know about lizards and where they live" or "I wonder how many kinds of reptiles there are").

Hold up the "Contents" page of the book (page 3). Show the "Contents" transparency and explain that this is the table of contents for this book. With the students, read the list of chapter titles. Then facilitate a whole-class discussion of the page by asking questions such as:

Q *What information about reptiles will you find in this book?*

Q *One thing you wanted to know about reptiles is [how many kinds of snakes there are]. Where might you find that information in* Reptiles?

3 ▶ Identify Other Features in *Reptiles*

Explain that the last four entries in the table of contents are found in the back of the book, and that each is a feature found in many expository texts. Turn to page 44 and point out that *Reptiles* has "To Find Out More" pages like *Morning Meals Around the World*. Remind the students that this section lists resources readers can use to find out more about a topic, including books, websites, and organizations.

Turn to page 46, and review the "Important Words" page. Then briefly mention the index (page 47), reminding students that it lists alphabetically the pages where readers can find information about specific topics. Also point out "Meet the Author" on page 48, which provides a brief biography of the author. Add this feature to the "Expository Text Features" chart.

4 ▶ Look for Features in Other Expository Texts

Ask the students to open to *Student Response Book* page 35, "Expository Text Features."

Teacher Note ▶

The students may need help naming features (for example, headings, subheadings, bold or italicized type, framed text, or colored text) and explaining how they are used.

Tell the students that you will give each pair an example of expository text and they will look through the text to see what features they can find. Some of the features will be the same as the ones in *Reptiles* and others will be different. (For example, they may see maps, charts, or diagrams.)

Distribute the texts you collected—one to each pair. Ask each pair to page through the text together, identifying the features in their book and discussing how each feature helps a reader make sense of the text. Then ask them to work together to list the features they identified on *Student Response Book* page 35.

CLASS COMPREHENSION ASSESSMENT

Circulate among the students as they work. Notice whether they are finding expository text features and whether they understand what information the features contribute. Ask yourself:

Q *Do the students recognize text features?*

Q *Do they have a sense of what information each feature contributes?*

Record your observations on page 21 of the *Assessment Resource Book*.

5 Discuss Features as a Class

When pairs are finished, facilitate a whole-class discussion of their findings. Refer to the "Expository Text Features" chart and ask:

Q *What features did you find that are already on the chart?*

Q *What features did you find that are not listed on the chart? How are they used?*

As the students mention a new feature, add it to the chart.

Save the "Expository Text Features" chart for the next lesson.

Reflect on Sharing Different Ideas

Facilitate a brief discussion about how the students shared different ideas. Ask:

Q *How was it sharing different ideas today? Why do you think it was helpful to share different ideas?*

INDIVIDUALIZED DAILY READING

Write About What They Know in Their IDR Journals/Read Independently

Prior to reading, ask the students to think about what they already know about the topics of their books and write that information in their IDR Journals.

Have the students read expository books independently for up to 30 minutes.

At the end of independent reading, have the students review what they wrote in their journals, add new information, and write what they would like to learn more about.

EXTENSION

Find and Discuss Features in Textbooks

Have partners look for text features in their science and social studies textbooks. As a class, discuss the text features and how they help the reader understand the information in the books. Encourage the students to look for and read the various text features in their textbooks.

Day 4

Guided Strategy Practice

In this lesson, the students:

- Identify and discuss features in expository texts
- Think about how text features add to the meaning of expository text
- Read independently for up to 30 minutes
- Share their thinking

Materials

- *Reptiles*
- "Expository Text Features" chart and a marker
- Expository texts at appropriate levels for independent reading
- *Student Response Book,* IDR Journal section

 1 Review Expository Text

Ask partners to sit together. Remind the students that this week they have continued to explore expository text while reading *Reptiles*. Refer to the "Expository Text Features" chart and remind them that they identified features of expository text. Ask:

Q *What have you learned about expository text this week?*

 2 Read and Discuss the Information on the Back of the Book and the Table of Contents

Make sure the students have a variety of expository texts at appropriate reading levels available to them. Explain that today they will read and explore text features in their own nonfiction books. Remind them that readers will often read the back of an expository text and the table of contents to find out what the book is about. Tell the students that they will read the information on the back of their books (if the book has information on the back cover) and the tables of contents; then they will talk in pairs about the topics of their books and what information they think they will find.

 After several minutes, have partners share the topics of their nonfiction books and what information they think they will find in the books.

◀ **Teacher Note**

This question gives you an opportunity to informally assess the students' learning this week. To gauge their understanding, you may need to ask follow-up questions such as:

Q *What is the purpose of expository text?*

Q *What features of expository text have we identified?*

Q *How does noticing features of expository text help us make sense of it?*

Ask questions such as:

Q *What is the topic of your book?*

Q *How did the summary on the back of the book and the table of contents help you know what your book is about?*

 Read the Index for Information

Explain that the students will read the index to find specific information in the book. Ask them to select a word or topic from the index, identify the pages where they will find the word, read those pages, and then share with their partners what they learned.

 After several minutes, have partners share the words or topics they selected and what information they read and anything they noticed about using the index.

As a class briefly discuss the following questions:

Q *What word or topic did you look up?*

Q *What information did you find out about [New York City]?*

Q *What did you notice about using the index of your book?*

Remind the students that readers use expository text features to help them find and understand information. Tell them that they should notice, use, and read text features during their independent reading.

Explain that in the coming weeks, the students will read and think more about other types of expository text.

Save the "Expository Text Features" chart for Week 3.

Reflect on Working Together

Facilitate a brief discussion about how the students worked together.

Ask:

Q *What did you like about how you worked together today? What problems did you have? How did you try to solve them?*

INDIVIDUALIZED DAILY READING

 Read Independently/Write About Text Features in Their IDR Journals

Explain that the students will read an expository text independently. Explain that as they read they will use their IDR Journals to record any text features they notice and what they learn from the features (for example, a student might write, "This diagram shows me the life cycle of a butterfly").

Have the students read independently for up to 30 minutes.

At the end of independent reading, have the students share what they wrote with their partners.

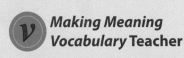
Making Meaning Vocabulary Teacher

Next week you will revisit *Reptiles* to teach Vocabulary Week 18.

Overview

UNIT 6: ANALYZING TEXT FEATURES

Expository Nonfiction

"Hop to It: Fancy Footwork"

This article traces the history of hopscotch and suggests variations to the traditional hopscotch game.

"Origami: The Art of Japanese Paper Folding"

This article gives a brief history of origami and describes the growing popularity and many uses of this art form.

"How to Make a Paper Airplane"

This functional text gives step-by-step instructions for making a paper airplane.

"Lincoln School Lunch Calendar for the week of May 21–25"

This functional text is a sample elementary school lunch calendar showing one week of menus.

ALTERNATIVE RESOURCES

Scholastic News, scholastic.com/news

Highlights Kids, highlightskids.com

Comprehension Focus

• Students identify what they learn from articles and functional texts.

• Students *explore text features* in articles.

• Students read independently.

Social Development Focus

• Students take responsibility for their learning and behavior.

D O A H E A D

• Prior to Day 3, make a chart entitled "Functional Texts at Our School."

• (Optional) Collect a variety of functional texts for the students to examine and read independently on Day 3.

• Make copies of the Unit 6 Parent Letter (BLM20) to send home with the students on the last day of the unit.

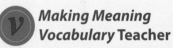

Making Meaning Vocabulary Teacher

If you are teaching Developmental Studies Center's *Making Meaning Vocabulary* program, teach Vocabulary Week 18 this week. For more information, see the *Making Meaning Vocabulary Teacher's Manual.*

Day 1

Materials

- "Hop to It" (see pages 316–317)
- "Reading Comprehension Strategies" chart
- *Student Response Book* pages 36–37
- Wall map of the world
- "Expository Text Features" chart and a marker

Read-aloud/Strategy Lesson

In this lesson, the students:

- *Explore text features* in expository texts
- Identify what they learn from an article
- Read independently for up to 30 minutes
- Take responsibility for their learning and behavior

▶1 Get Ready to Work Together

Have partners sit together. Remind the students that they have been working on listening carefully to what their partners say and contributing different ideas to their partner discussions. Encourage the students to continue to practice these skills, and explain that this week they also will notice how they take responsibility for their behavior and learning. Ask the students to pay particular attention to how they take responsibility for their behavior today.

▶2 Review Recognizing Text Features and Introduce "Hop to It: Fancy Footwork"

Remind the students that during the last two weeks they explored a kind of nonfiction called expository text. They heard expository nonfiction books and used text features to help them understand the books. Refer to the "Reading Comprehension Strategies" chart and review that *recognizing text features* is a comprehension strategy readers use to help them make sense of expository text.

Explain that this week the students will use text features to help them understand articles. Articles might appear in newspapers, magazines, or on websites. Ask and briefly discuss:

Q *What newspapers, magazines, or websites have you seen or read?*

Explain that the article you will read aloud today was written by a company that publishes news magazines for young readers. Read the title aloud: "Hop to It: Fancy Footwork." Explain that the article describes hopscotch around the world.

Explain to the students that as you read you want the students to listen for how hopscotch is played around the world. Tell them that you will stop during the reading so partners can talk about the article.

 ## 3 Read Aloud

Have the students turn to pages 36–37 in their *Student Response Books* and explain that this is a copy of the article you will be reading. Tell the students that the first part of the article explains how the game of hopscotch started and how its popularity spread around the world. Explain that you will read the first part twice and ask them to follow along in their *Student Response Books*.

Read the first two paragraphs and "Hopping Around the World," stopping to point out the countries and continents mentioned in the article on a wall map of the world. Reread the first two sections aloud, and stop after:

> **p. 317** "For example, in Alaska, the squares are not named or numbered."

Suggested Vocabulary

training exercise: something you do to make your body stronger (p. 316)

ELL Vocabulary

English Language Learners may benefit from discussing additional vocabulary, including:

courts: special places for playing a game (p. 316)

imitated: copied (p. 316)

popular: many people like it (p. 317)

children changed the game their own way: children played the game in different ways (p. 317)

 First in pairs, and then as a class, discuss:

Q *What have you found out about the game of hopscotch so far?*

 Teacher Note

Before reading the article aloud, make sure the students are familiar with the game of hopscotch. If they are not, draw a picture of a traditional hopscotch court and read "How to Play" on page 316 aloud.

 ELL Note

To support your English Language Learners, you may want to read the article aloud and check for understanding, prior to the class read-aloud.

Have the students follow along in their *Student Response Books* as you continue reading "Hopping in France" and "An Alaskan Pastime."

4 ▶ Discuss the Article

Ask:

Q *What did you find out about hopscotch from this article?*

 Use "Turn to Your Partner" to have the students discuss:

Q *What is one thing you found out about hopscotch that surprised you?*

Have a few volunteers share their thinking.

5 ▶ Discuss Text Features

Call the students' attention to the different hopscotch court diagrams and read the accompanying captions aloud. Ask and briefly discuss:

Q *How do these diagrams help you understand the article?*

Students might say:

"You can see what the hopscotch courts look like."

"In addition to what [Paula] said, It shows how the courts are different for hopscotch in different places."

"When I look at the diagram, I can picture playing the game in my mind."

Explain that diagrams are a text feature often found in articles and other kinds of expository nonfiction. Add *diagrams* to the "Expository Text Features" chart.

Explain that tomorrow the students will hear another article and look at more text features.

FACILITATION TIP

Reflect on your experience during the past few weeks with **avoiding repeating or paraphrasing** students' responses. Is the practice beginning to feel natural? Are you integrating it into class discussions throughout the day? What effect is it having on the students? Are they participating more responsibly in discussions? We encourage you to continue to try this practice and reflect on students' responses as you continue to facilitate class discussions.

Expository
Text Features

- summary on the back
  of the book

Reflect on Taking Responsibility

Ask and briefly discuss:

Q *How did you take responsibility for your behavior today? Why is that important to do?*

INDIVIDUALIZED DAILY READING

Document IDR Conferences/Review Reading Comprehension Strategies

Review the strategies on the "Reading Comprehension Strategies" chart with the students. Ask the students to notice which strategies they use during IDR today.

Have the students read independently for up to 30 minutes.

Use the "IDR Conference Notes" record sheet to conduct and document individual conferences.

At the end of IDR, have several students share with the class the reading comprehension strategies they used. Have each volunteer share the strategy he used and when he used it. Ask the students to explain how the strategies helped them make sense of the text they were reading.

> *Reading Comprehension Strategies*
>
> *- making connections*

EXTENSION

Play Hopscotch

Reread "Hop to It: Fancy Footwork" aloud as the students follow along in their *Student Response Books*. Encourage the students to try the different variations of hopscotch at recess. Ask the students to report on which version they liked the best and why.

Hop to It Fancy Footwork

Looking for a fun outdoor game? Grab a piece of chalk, a stone, and a friend. What can you play? Hopscotch!

The first hopscotch courts were made around 2,000 years ago. Imagine a hopscotch court 100 feet long—about the length of a professional basketball court. That's how big the first courts were. They were not made for fun, either. Instead, they were used for a training exercise. Roman soldiers dressed in heavy armor ran from one end of the court to the other and back again. This exercise helped them stay quick on their feet.

A traditional hopscotch court has eight or ten squares. Once you have learned how to play and how to hop on one leg, it's a lot of fun.

How to Play

To play a game of traditional hopscotch, all you need is one traditional hopscotch court (you can draw one with chalk), one stone, and two or more people. Make sure all the players know these rules:

- A player must toss the stone into every square in sequence.
- Players can only land in any square on one foot.
- Players can't land on a line.
- Players can't hop into any square holding the stone.
- A player's turn ends if he or she breaks any of the above rules or if the stone doesn't land in the right square when it is tossed.

When it's your turn, you toss the stone into square 1 and then hop on one leg into square 2. Next, jump into squares 3 and 4 so that your left foot is in square 3 and your right foot is in square 4. Now continue to hop and jump to the end of the court (making sure only one foot lands in each square!). Now, turn around in the "home" square and hop back to the beginning of the court, pausing to pick up the stone in square 1 before you hop out.

Once you've completed the first pass through the court, toss the stone into square 2 and hop the court again, hopping over the square that has your stone in it. Continue throwing your stone into the next square and hopping the court until you step on a line or fall. Then it's the next player's turn! When it's your turn again, you continue by tossing the stone into the last square you aimed for. The first player who is able to complete hopping the course with his or her stone in the last square is the winner!

Hopping Around the World

Roman children watched the soldiers and imitated them. They drew smaller courts on the ground with chalk and they made their own rules. Hopscotch became a game! Their game was simple to learn, yet challenging to play. It quickly became popular, spreading through Europe. Later, it spread to Asia and America.

In every country, children changed the game their own way. In France, the court is drawn in the shape of a snail. In Bolivia, the squares in the court are named for the days of the week. In the U.S., hopscotch is played in many ways. For example, in Alaska, the squares are not named or numbered.

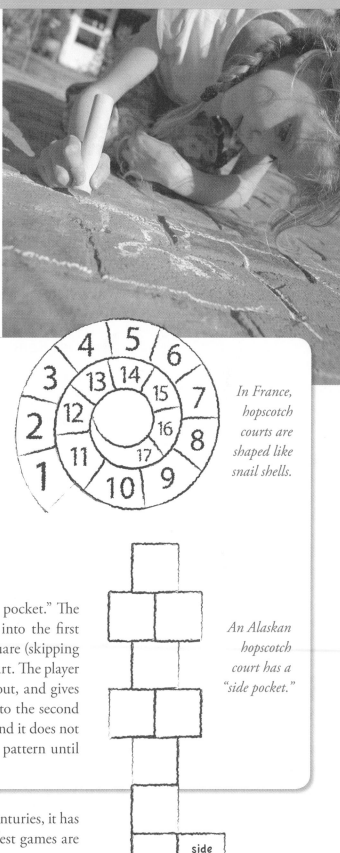

Hopping in France

In the French hopscotch game, no stone is used. The player hops through the spiral shape, from square 1 to square 17. Then the player hops back to the beginning, chooses a square, and writes his or her name inside it. The other players must hop over this square. The game is over when it becomes too hard for anyone to hop to the center. The player whose name is written inside the most squares is the winner.

In France, hopscotch courts are shaped like snail shells.

An Alaskan Pastime

In the Alaskan version of hopscotch, the court has a "side pocket." The player stands inside the side pocket and tosses the stone into the first square. The player then hops diagonally into the second square (skipping the square holding the stone), and hops to the end of the court. The player hops back to the second square, picks up the stone, hops out, and gives the stone to the next player. That player tosses the stone into the second square and repeats the pattern. If a player tosses the stone and it does not land in a square, that player is out. The players repeat the pattern until one person is left—the winner!

An Alaskan hopscotch court has a "side pocket."

Hopscotch is a simple game with a long history. Over the centuries, it has spread all over the world. Hopscotch proves that the simplest games are often the most popular.

Materials

- "Origami" (see pages 322–323)
- *Student Response Book* pages 38–39
- "Expository Text Features" chart and a marker

Read-aloud/Strategy Lesson

In this lesson, the students:

- *Explore text features* in expository texts
- Identify what they learn from an article
- Read independently for up to 30 minutes
- Take responsibility for their learning and behavior

1 ▶ Get Ready to Work Together

Have partners sit together. Remind the students that they are noticing when they take responsibility for their behavior and learning. Without naming names, mention a few examples you've noticed of students taking responsibility for themselves. Ask the students to continue to notice when they are being responsible.

2 ▶ Preview "Origami: The Art of Japanese Paper Folding" Using Text Features

Review that yesterday the students heard and read part of the article "Hop to It: Fancy Footwork" and thought about what they learned from the text features in the article. Today they will hear and read another article and look at other text features readers can use to help them make sense of nonfiction.

 Note

Preview the article with your English Language Learners prior to today's read-aloud. Stop frequently to make sure the students understand the text.

Explain that the article the students will hear today is about a special way of folding paper called origami. Have them turn to *Student Response Book* pages 38–39 and explain that this is a copy of the article. Draw their attention to the article title and headings and point out that they are in bold print so readers can find them easily. Explain that the title and headings are text features that help readers know what information might be in an article.

Have the students follow along in their *Student Response Books* as you read the title and section headings aloud; then ask and briefly discuss:

Q *After reading the title and section headings, what do you think you might learn from this article?*

Have a few volunteers share their thinking.

> **Students might say:**
>
> "It might tell where origami came from."
>
> "I agree with [Chris], and you might find out how to make things with origami."
>
> "The article might tell about origami around the world."

Draw the students' attention to the map in the article and explain that origami is an art form popular in Japan, a country in Asia. Point out that maps give readers more information about important places mentioned in expository nonfiction.

Add *title*, *headings*, and *maps* to the "Expository Text Features" chart.

◀ **Teacher Note**

If the students have difficulty answering the question, offer some suggestions like those in the "Students might say" note.

Expository Text Features

- *summary on the back of the book*

3 ▶ Read "Origami: The Art of Japanese Paper Folding" Aloud

Read the article aloud, having the students follow along in their *Student Response Books* and stopping as described on the next page. At each stop, use "Turn to Your Partner" to have the students discuss what they learned in the part they heard.

Suggested Vocabulary

temples: buildings where people go to pray or worship (p. 322)
creases: folds (p. 323)
unusual-looking life-forms: strange creatures (p. 323)
Massachusetts Institute of Technology: a famous college (p. 323)

ELL Vocabulary

English Language Learners may benefit from discussing additional vocabulary, including:

geometry: kind of math that has to do with shapes (p. 322)
objects: things or pieces (p. 322)

Stop after:

p. 322 "Japanese students also use origami at school to help them understand geometry."

p. 323 "Another artist, Chris Alexander, makes paper spaceships and other unusual shapes."

Reread the last sentence and continue reading to the end of the article. (Skip the information in the "One Thousand Paper Cranes" text box. You will read this after discussing the article.)

 Discuss the Article

Ask and briefly discuss:

Q *What did you find out about origami from this article?*

Q *What is something you would like to make with origami?*

 Read the "One Thousand Paper Cranes" Text Box

Direct the students' attention to the text box on page 39 of their *Student Response Books* and have them follow along as you read it aloud.

Point out that text boxes such as this one often tell a story related to the article or give readers more information about the topic. Add *text box* to the "Expository Text Features" chart.

Explain that tomorrow the students will look at a different kind of expository nonfiction and talk about it with their partners and as a class.

ELL Note

You might prompt the students to begin their responses by saying, "I found out…" and "I would like to make…."

INDIVIDUALIZED DAILY READING

6 ▶ **Read Independently/Discuss the Strategies They Use to Make Sense of Their Texts**

Have the students independently read expository texts for up to 30 minutes. Ask the students to pay attention to the comprehension strategies they are using as they read.

 At the end of IDR, have partners share which strategies they used and how the strategies helped them understand what they read.

Origami

THE ART OF JAPANESE PAPER FOLDING

Could you fold a square of paper into a graceful fish or a long-stemmed flower? Origami, or Japanese paper folding, is an art form practiced by many people. In origami, a simple sheet of paper can become a spectacular piece of art.

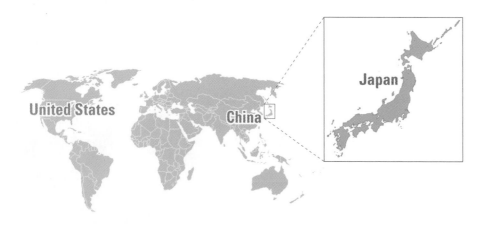

Japan is an island country that lies near the east coasts of Russia, Korea, and China. It is made up of four major islands and is one of the most crowded countries in the world.

Ancient Art Form, Modern Appeal

Origami began in ancient China and spread to Japan in the early 700s. At first, people made paper decorations to hang inside temples. Then, women began to make paper toys and dolls for their children, and it became popular to make paper models as a hobby. People folded simple shapes from nature, such as butterflies, flowers, and fish. Today, children learn origami from their parents or grandparents. Japanese students also use origami at school to help them understand geometry.

Traditionally, origami objects are created using square pieces of very thin paper that range in size from 1 to 6 inches wide. The paper is usually colored or patterned on one or both sides. The paper square is not cut or glued, but is shaped by making a series of creases and folds. Some artists use wet paper to achieve a more rounded look; others experiment with unusual materials, such as cloth, wire, sheet metal, and even pasta.

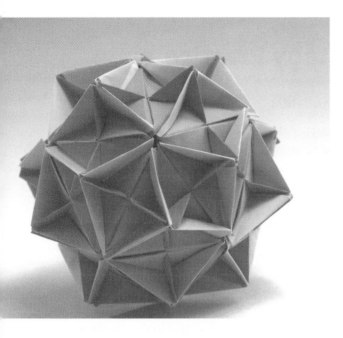

Folding origami can be a fun challenge. Some complicated origami figures are constructed using several sheets of paper.

A Worldwide Craze

As people from Asia moved to the West, origami became more popular in Europe and the United States. Today, there are fans of origami worldwide. The most popular shapes are still traditional Japanese models, such as flowers and birds, but many people are inspired by more unusual-looking life-forms, such as scorpions, armadillos, and horned beetles. One young American artist, Jake Crowley, makes models of cartoon characters. Another artist, Chris Alexander, makes paper spaceships and other unusual shapes.

Some people submit their paper creations in origami contests. In an origami contest, there are categories such as smallest, largest, and most original models. You will see creations such as frogs as tiny as a fingernail, life-sized dinosaurs, and origami you can wear. In 2006, a student won an origami contest at the Massachusetts Institute of Technology for his original gold-colored model of a beaver.

Origami is a tradition that has been passed on through many generations. Artists fold origami to express themselves. Scientists and architects use it to explore shapes and angles. Teachers use origami as a tool to help people learn. And many people fold paper just because it's fun.

One Thousand Paper Cranes

In the city of Hiroshima, Japan, children bring thousands of paper cranes to a memorial park every year. They do this to remember a girl named Sadako Sasaki. During World War II (1939–1945), Sadako became ill with radiation sickness. She had heard the tradition that if a sick person folds one thousand paper cranes, he or she will become healthy again.

Sadako decided to fold one thousand paper cranes, but she died with three hundred cranes still to make. Her friends completed the last paper cranes for her. Sadako's determination to finish her project has come to stand for a wish for peace. Today, people across the world fold paper cranes and string them onto chains. They send them to the memorial park to remember Sadako's dream.

A one-thousand-crane chain takes a long time for one person to make, but it can be completed quickly if many people join in.

Day 3

Materials

- Scratch paper and a pencil
- "Functional Texts at Our School" chart, prepared ahead, and a marker
- (Optional) A variety of functional texts that students can examine and read independently
- (Optional) *Student Response Book* pages 40–41

Teacher Note ▶

Other examples of functional texts are tickets, bills, menus, receipts, calendars, and food wrappers.

Teacher Note ▶

If the students have difficulty answering the question, offer some suggestions like those in the "Students might say" note.

Guided Strategy Practice

In this lesson, the students:

- Look for and read functional texts inside and outside the classroom
- Identify what they learn from functional texts
- Read independently for up to 30 minutes
- Move around the school responsibly

1 ▶ **Review Articles and Introduce Functional Texts**

Review that this week the students heard and read articles about hopscotch and origami and thought about how expository text features help readers understand articles. Today the students will explore another kind of expository nonfiction called functional texts.

Explain that functional texts help readers do things in everyday life. Some examples of functional texts are street signs, labels, posters, recipes, instructions, and schedules.

 Point out one or two functional texts in the classroom; then use "Turn to Your Partner" to have the students discuss:

Q *What other functional texts do you see in our classroom?*

Have several volunteers point out the functional text they noticed. As they share, briefly discuss how the functional text is helpful.

> **Students might say:**
>
> "I see the class meeting rules. Having the rules posted reminds us to follow them."
>
> "The name tags on our desks help us learn everyone's name."
>
> "The map on our bulletin board lets us know how to leave the classroom if there is a fire."

Introduce the School Walk

Explain that today the class will take a walk around the school to look for functional texts. Explain that during the walk you will stop a few times so the students can look around and talk about the functional texts they see. Remind the students how you expect them to behave on the walk. (For example, you might say, "I expect you to walk with your partner. I expect you to watch me for signals about when to stop, listen, and talk. When you talk to your partner, I expect you to whisper.")

Ask and briefly discuss:

Q *What people do we want to be considerate of when we walk around outside the classroom? Why do we want to be considerate of them?*

Q *What can we do so we don't disturb other classes when we walk around?*

> **Students might say:**
>
> "We want to be considerate of kids in other classes."
>
> "It's important to be considerate so we don't bother people."
>
> "We can be considerate if we pass the principal in the hall. We can smile at her."
>
> "We can not stomp our feet really loud when we walk."

Ask the students to keep in mind what they talked about, and tell them that you will check in with them after the walk to see how they did.

 Take a Class Walk Around the School

Lead the students on a walk around the school. Bring paper and a pencil with you to jot down the their observations. At the first stop, ask:

 Q *What functional texts do you see? Turn and whisper to your partner.*

◀ **Teacher Note**

You might take the students to the office, library, nurse's office, or to another public space on the campus. If a walk around the school is not possible, you might provide a variety of functional texts that the students can examine in class or use the sample functional texts on *Student Response Book* pages 40–41.

Signal for the students' attention and have a couple of students quietly share their observations. If necessary, share one or two functional texts you notice. (For example, you might say, "I notice the lunch schedule and the exit sign.") Jot down functional texts the students mention. After a few students have shared, continue the walk, stopping to notice functional texts in other areas of the school.

4 ▶ List Functional Texts as a Class

 When you return to the classroom, have partners sit together. Use "Turn to Your Partner" to have them discuss:

Q *What functional texts did you see on our walk?*

As volunteers share with the class, record functional texts they mention on the "Functional Texts at Our School" chart. Help the students think about the purposes of functional texts by asking follow-up questions, such as:

Q *What information does [the lunch menu] give you?*

Q *How does the ["In Case of Emergency" poster] help us?*

Explain that tomorrow the students will look at more functional texts and talk about how the information they provide is helpful to readers.

5 ▶ Reflect on How the Students Acted Responsibly During the School Walk

Ask and briefly discuss:

Q *What did you do to act in a responsible way during the walk? How do you think that helped the people around us?*

Q *What problems, if any, did we have? What can we do next time to avoid those problems?*

INDIVIDUALIZED DAILY READING

 Document IDR Conferences/Discuss Text Features

Have the students read expository texts for up to 30 minutes.

Use the "IDR Conference Notes" record sheet to conduct and document individual conferences.

At the end of IDR, discuss the text features the students noticed. Ask questions such as:

Q *What is your book about?*

Q *What text features does your book have? What did you learn from those features?*

Q *What information did you get from the table of contents about the topic of your book?*

 Note

Have your English Language Learners ask themselves these questions as they read independently.

EXTENSION

Share Examples of Functional Texts

Have the students bring in examples of functional texts from their daily lives. Have them point out the features in the examples and explain how the features help readers. If appropriate, have pairs glue their examples to a large sheet of construction paper and label each example and its features and uses. (For example, a weather graph from the newspaper might be labeled "newspaper weather graph, gives weather predictions for the next five days.")

Day 4

Materials

- "How to Make a Paper Airplane" (see page 333)
- "Lincoln School Lunch Calendar for the week of May 21–25" (see page 334)
- *Student Response Book* pages 42–43
- "Functional Texts at Our School" chart from Day 3
- "Expository Text Features" chart from Day 2 and a marker
- "Reading Comprehension Strategies" chart
- *Assessment Resource Book*
- Unit 6 Parent Letter (BLM20)

Read-aloud/Strategy Lesson

In this lesson, the students:

- Identify what they learn from functional texts
- Explore the organization of functional texts
- Read independently for up to 30 minutes
- Take responsibility for their learning and behavior

 ## Review Functional Texts

Have partners sit together. Refer to the "Functional Texts at Our School" chart and remind the students that yesterday they explored functional texts in the classroom and around the school. Review that functional texts are a type of expository nonfiction that help readers do things in everyday life.

Explain that today the students will look closely at two functional texts and discuss how they help readers.

Introduce and Read Aloud "How to Make a Paper Airplane"

Have the students turn to page 42 in their *Student Response Books*. Read the title "How to Make a Paper Airplane" aloud, and explain that these are directions for making a paper airplane. Explain that a set of directions for making something is a type of functional text.

Ask the students to follow along as you read the directions for making the airplane and the "Flying Tips" aloud, giving the students a moment to look at the diagram for each step before reading the next step.

Suggested Vocabulary

vertically: straight up and down (p. 333)

align: line up (p. 333)

Give pairs a few moments to look over the directions together, and then have them discuss:

Q *What makes these directions easy to use?*

Have volunteers share.

> **Students might say:**
>
> "The steps are numbered so you know what to do first."
>
> "There are pictures to show you how to fold the plane."
>
> "In addition to what [Luz] said, it tells you what the different parts of the plane are, like the wings and the rudder."

Point out that the numbered steps and labeled diagrams are expository text features that make this functional text easy for readers to use. Add *numbered steps* and *labeled diagrams* to the "Expository Text Features" chart.

 3 **Introduce and Read Aloud "Lincoln School Lunch Calendar for the week of May 21–25"**

Explain that the students will look at another kind of functional text, and have them turn to page 43 in their *Student Response Books.* Read the title "Lincoln School Lunch Calendar for the week of May 21–25" aloud and explain that this is a calendar showing school lunch menus for one week. Call the students' attention to the legend and explain that it gives readers extra information without making the calendar too crowded.

Ask the students to follow along as you read the calendar aloud, referring to the legend as necessary.

ELL Vocabulary

English Language Learners may benefit from discussing the following vocabulary:

vegetarian sandwich: sandwich made with vegetables, not meat (p. 334)

nuggets: small pieces (p. 334)

Have the students think about the following question as they reread the calendar quietly to themselves.

Q *What information does this calendar give you?*

 After a few moments, call for the students' attention and have partners talk about what information they found in the calendar.

CLASS COMPREHENSION ASSESSMENT

Circulate among the students as they work. Randomly select students to observe and ask yourself:

Q *Are the students able to identify what they learn from the functional text?*

Q *Are students noticing and making sense of text features?*

Record your observations on page 22 of the *Assessment Resource Book*.

Have several volunteers share.

 Use "Turn to Your Partner" to have the students discuss:

Q *What makes this calendar easy to use?*

Students might say:

"The title has the dates in it so you know which week it's for."

"It says the days of the week at the top."

"The menu for each day is in its own box."

Point out that the title, column headings, and legend are expository text features that help make it easy for readers to find information in the calendar. Add *titles*, *column headings*, and *legends* to the "Expository Text Features" chart.

Explain that because the lunch calendar and the instructions for the paper airplane give different information, they are organized in different ways to help the reader make sense of them. Tell the students that reading functional texts carefully and noticing how they are organized helps readers understand and use them more easily. Encourage the students to continue to notice functional texts in their everyday lives.

4 Review Recognizing Text Features and Reflect on Working with a Partner

Review that in the past few weeks the students have explored and discussed expository text features in books and articles and looked closely at functional texts. Refer to the "Reading Comprehension Strategies" chart and review that recognizing text features is a comprehension strategy readers use to help them make sense of expository text. Tell the students that recognizing and reading text features can help them understand what they read at a deeper level. Draw their attention to the "Expository Text Features" chart, and encourage them to use expository text features to help them understand what they read.

Explain to the students that this is the last lesson in which they will work with their current partners. Facilitate a brief discussion about how they took responsibility working with their partners and how they plan to take responsibility for their behavior when they work with their new partners.

Save the "Expository Text Features" chart for use in Unit 7.

Teacher Note

This is the last week of Unit 6. You will assign new partners for Unit 7.

INDIVIDUALIZED DAILY READING

5 Read Independently

Have the students read independently for up to 30 minutes.

At the end of IDR, have partners share with one another the parts of their books that they found the most interesting. Remind the students to tell one another what their books are about.

Circulate as partners discuss their books and ask individual students questions such as:

Q   *What is your book about?*

Q   *What part of your book is the most interesting to you? Why?*

Q   *What more would you like to learn about [ballet dancers]?*

 Note

Before your English Language Learners read independently, preview the questions you plan to ask them at the end of independent reading.

INDIVIDUAL COMPREHENSION ASSESSMENT

Before continuing with Unit 7, take this opportunity to assess individual students' progress in recognizing text features to help them make sense of their reading. Please refer to pages 38–39 in the *Assessment Resource Book* for instructions.

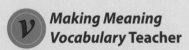

Parent Letter

Send home with each student the Parent Letter for this unit (see "Do Ahead," page 311). Periodically, have a few students share with the class what they are reading at home.

Making Meaning Vocabulary Teacher

Next week you will revisit "Origami" to teach Vocabulary Week 19.

How to Make
A PAPER AIRPLANE

1. Fold the sheet of paper in half vertically. Open the paper.

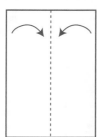

2. Fold the top left-hand and right-hand corners down so that they align with the center fold and form triangles.

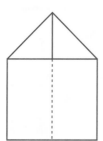

3. Fold the side left- and right-hand corners down so that they align with the center fold and again form triangles.

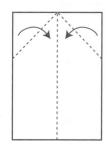

4. Fold the paper in half by folding the left side under the right.

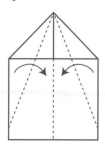

5. Fold the top wing in half so that it aligns with the rudder.

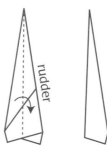

6. Flip the plane over and fold the other wing in half so that it aligns with the rudder.

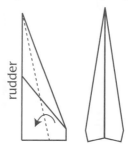

7. Open plane and fold the wing tips up to help the plane fly better.

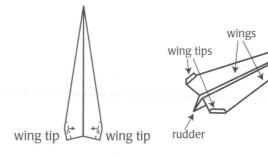

Flying Tips:

- If your plane dives and crashes, fold the back edges of the wings up a little.
- If your plane flies too far to the right, bend the rudder a little to the left.
- If your plane flies too far to the left, bend the rudder a little to the right.

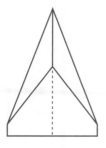
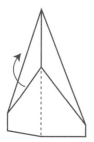

Lincoln School Lunch Calendar

for the week of May 21–25

Monday	Tuesday	Wednesday	Thursday	Friday
21st	**22nd**	**23rd**	**24th**	**25th**
• "Homemade" ham and cheese sandwiches with lettuce and tomato* or Vegetarian sandwiches** • Carnival crunch • Fruit cup	• "Homemade" turkey, mashed potatoes, gravy • Mixed green salad with veggie sticks on top • Fresh fruit	• Fish nuggets with dip or Cheese sticks with dip** • Aloha dinner roll • Low-fat ice cream or Strawberries with yogurt dip	• "Homemade" lasagna with meat sauce and vegetable or Vegetarian lasagna** • Italian breadstick • Fresh fruit	• Pizza: pepperoni* or cheese** • Vegetable sticks with dip • Fruit cup

*contains pork
**vegetarian selection

$10.00 milk ticket (20 cartons)
$0.50 student a la carte milk

$3.00 daily lunch price
$0.40 reduced price

Unit 7

Wondering/ Questioning

EXPOSITORY NONFICTION

During this unit, the students identify what they learn from nonfiction texts, including articles, and use wondering/questioning and schema to make sense of nonfiction. During IDR, the students use questioning to help them make sense of their independent reading. Socially, they develop the group skill of asking clarifying questions and reflect on how they are taking responsibility for their behavior.

Week 1 *Flashy Fantastic Rain Forest Frogs*
by Dorothy Hinshaw Patent

Week 2 *What Is a Bat?* by Bobbie Kalman and Heather Levigne

Week 3 "Why Do Animals Play?" by Kathleen Weidner Zoehfeld
"Feeling the Heat" by Kathryn R. Satterfield
"Banning Tag"

UNIT 7: WONDERING/QUESTIONING
Expository Nonfiction

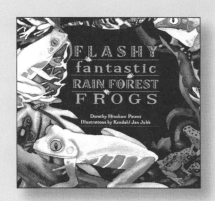

Flashy Fantastic Rain Forest Frogs
by Dorothy Hinshaw Patent, illustrated by Kendahl Jan Jubb
(Walker, 1999)

Readers learn about the appearance, diet, life cycle, and unique characteristics of the many species of rain forest frogs.

ALTERNATIVE BOOKS

The Right Dog for the Job by Dorothy Hinshaw Patent

Building an Igloo by Ulli Steltzer

Comprehension Focus

• Students use *wondering/questioning* to make sense of nonfiction texts.

• Students *use schema* to make sense of nonfiction texts.

• Students read independently.

Social Development Focus

• Students analyze why it is important to be caring and respectful.

• Students develop the group skill of asking clarifying questions.

DO AHEAD

• Prior to Day 1, decide how you will randomly assign partners to work together during the unit.

• Prepare a chart with the title "Questions to Help Me Understand My Partner" (for Days 1–2).

• Prepare a chart with the title "Things We Wonder About *Flashy Fantastic Rain Forest Frogs*" (for Days 1–4).

• Select an expository book and prepare to model wondering on Day 4 (see Day 4, Step 2 on page 352).

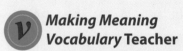

Making Meaning Vocabulary Teacher

If you are teaching Developmental Studies Center's *Making Meaning Vocabulary* program, teach Vocabulary Week 19 this week. For more information, see the *Making Meaning Vocabulary Teacher's Manual.*

Day 1

Materials

- *Flashy Fantastic Rain Forest Frogs* (pages 3–9)

- "Questions to Help Me Understand My Partner" chart, prepared ahead, and a marker

- "Things We Wonder About *Flashy Fantastic Rain Forest Frogs*" chart, prepared ahead, and a marker

- "Expository Text Features" chart (from Unit 6)

Being a Writer™ Teacher

You can either have the students work with their *Being a Writer* partner or assign them a different partner for the *Making Meaning* lessons.

Read-aloud

In this lesson, the students:

- *Use schema* to articulate all they think they know about a topic before they read

- *Wonder* about a text

- Identify what they learn from the text

- Read independently for up to 30 minutes

- Ask clarifying questions

1 ▶ Introduce Asking Clarifying Questions

Randomly assign new partners and have them sit together. Remind the students that in previous weeks they focused on contributing ideas that are different from their partners' ideas. Explain that this week they will focus on a new skill for working with a partner—asking questions when they don't understand what their partners say.

Explain that when a student doesn't understand what her partner means, she can ask questions that will help clarify, or make clear, what her partner is saying. Model a clarifying question or two for the students (for example, "Sometimes when one of you is talking to me and I don't understand you, I'll say, 'I'm not sure I understand you. Can you say that in a different way?'"). Write your example on the "Questions to Help Me Understand My Partner" chart. Then ask:

Q *If you don't understand your partner, what are some questions you can ask to help you understand what [he] is saying?*

Add the students' suggestions to the chart. Tell them that today you would like them to use these questions when they don't understand their partner. Explain that at the end of the lesson you will ask them to report how they did with using the questions. Point out that they can also use the questions when they don't understand something you have said.

Teacher Note

If the students have trouble suggesting clarifying questions, provide a few more examples to stimulate their thinking (for example, "Can you tell me more about that?" "What did you mean when you said…?" "Can you give me an example of what you mean?"). Emphasize that it is important to speak politely and respectfully when seeking clarification.

Introduce *Flashy Fantastic Rain Forest Frogs*

Explain that this week the students will continue to look at expository text—text that explains or gives information. Review that expository texts include features, like photos with captions, that give readers additional information and help them understand the text.

Tell the students that today you will read aloud from a book called *Flashy Fantastic Rain Forest Frogs*. Show the cover of the book and read the title and the names of the author and illustrator. Show pages 3–5, and point out that the book contains text and illustrations, but not photographs, captions, or other features found in other expository texts they have read this year. Explain that it is still an expository text because it gives information about a topic— rain forest frogs.

Show the illustration on page 4 again and explain that rain forests are forests with thickly growing plants and trees. They are located in warm parts of the earth where a lot of rain falls. Many different kinds of animals, including monkeys, parrots, leopards, crocodiles, and frogs, live in rain forests. Ask and briefly discuss:

Q *What do you think you know about frogs?*

Q *Based on what you think you know about frogs, what do you wonder about frogs that live in rain forests?*

List a few students' responses to the second question on the "Things We Wonder About *Flashy Fantastic Rain Forest Frogs*" chart. Write each response as an "I wonder..." statement. (For example, a student might say, "I wonder if rain forest frogs are like the frogs that live around here.") Explain that after you read the first part of the book today the students will discuss these ideas and what they learned from the reading.

 Read Aloud with Brief Section Introductions

Tell the students that the first page you will read describes the many different kinds of rain forest frogs. Ask them to listen for information they didn't know before.

 Note

Your English Language Learners will benefit from previewing the book prior to today's read-aloud. In addition, you may want to show your students photos of other animals that live in rain forests.

Suggested Vocabulary

flashy: brightly colored (p. 3)

tropical: having to do with hot, rainy areas of the world known as the tropics (p. 5)

cling: hold on tightly (p. 6)

blend perfectly with: look just like (p. 9)

ELL Vocabulary

English Language Learners may benefit from discussing additional vocabulary, including:

ordinary: usual (p. 3)

moist: wet (p. 3)

freezes: becomes very cold; is icy (p. 5)

Read page 3 and show the illustration. Stop after:

> **p. 3** "The males croak to attract females, which then lay eggs without shells."

Ask:

Q *Based on what you've heard, what are you wondering?*

Have the students use "Turn to Your Partner" to talk about their ideas. Remind them to ask questions if they don't understand their partners' thinking. After a few minutes, have two or three students share with the class. Add these ideas to the "Things We Wonder About *Flashy Fantastic Rain Forest Frogs*" chart.

> *Students might say:*
>
> "I wonder where frogs as big as my thumb live in the rain forest."
>
> "I wonder if there are blue and orange frogs in other places besides in the rain forest."
>
> "I wonder what makes the frogs so colorful."

Explain that the next part you will read describes the rain forest. Read and show the illustration on page 5 and stop after:

> **p. 5** "The forest floor is shaded by the plants above, so, often, little grows there."

▶ Teacher Note

In Unit 4, the students were introduced to *wondering/questioning* and used the strategy to make meaning of narrative fiction. In Unit 5, the students used *wondering/questioning* to explore narrative nonfiction. During the next three weeks, they will use the strategy to explore expository text, including articles.

Again, ask:

Q *Based on what you've heard, what are you wondering?*

 Have the students use "Turn to Your Partner" to discuss their thinking. After a few moments, have two or three students share with the class and add these ideas to the chart. Tell the students that the last part you will read today tells where frogs live in the rain forest and what they eat. Read pages 6–9, showing the illustrations, and stop after:

> **p. 9** "They can eat almost anything that comes their way, even mice and small rats."

Follow the procedure you used at the previous stops, including adding the students' "I wonder" statements to the chart.

▶ 4 Discuss the Reading and "I Wonder" Statements

 First in pairs, and then as a class, have the students discuss things they wondered and whether what they wondered is addressed in the book. Be ready to reread passages aloud and show illustrations again to help the students recall what they heard. Ask:

Q *What ideas that you wondered about are discussed in the book?*

Q *What did you learn about where frogs live in the rain forest?*

Explain that tomorrow you will read more from *Flashy Fantastic Rain Forest Frogs* and they will listen to find out if their "I wonder" statements that have not been addressed so far are discussed in the next part of the book.

▶ 5 Discuss Asking Clarifying Questions

Facilitate a brief discussion about how the students did asking clarifying questions. Ask:

Q *Did you or your partner have trouble understanding each other at any point?*

Refer to the "Questions to Help Me Understand My Partner" chart.

Q *How did asking these questions help you understand each other better?*

Tell the students that they will continue to practice this skill in the next lesson.

Save the "Questions to Help Me Understand My Partner" chart for Day 2.

INDIVIDUALIZED DAILY READING

6 **Review Previewing a Text Before Reading/ Read Independently**

Refer to the "Expository Text Features" chart and review that these features help the reader make sense of the text. Tell the students that looking at the cover, reading the information on the back of the book, and previewing the book by looking through the pages is particularly helpful when reading expository text. Ask the students to take the time to do this today before starting to read even if they are already partway through a book.

Have the students read expository nonfiction books at appropriate reading levels independently for up to 30 minutes.

As the students read, circulate and stop and ask individual students questions such as:

Q *What did you notice about your book from looking it over before reading? How is this helpful to you?*

Q *What are some features in your book? What questions do you have about them?*

Q *If you don't understand what you are reading, what strategies are you using?*

Expository
Text Features

- summary on the back of the book

Q *Are you finding the whole book confusing or just this part?*
(If it's just this section) *Let's go back and reread a little together and see what strategies you might use.*
(If the whole book is confusing) *Let me help you find another book that might be a better choice for you right now.*

At the end of independent reading, have a few students share with the class what they learned by previewing their books before they read. Encourage the students to look their books over whenever they choose a new expository book to read.

Day 2

Materials

- *Flashy Fantastic Rain Forest Frogs* (pages 10–15 and 27)
- "Questions to Help Me Understand My Partner" chart from Day 1
- "Things We Wonder About *Flashy Fantastic Rain Forest Frogs*" chart from Day 1 and a marker

---

Questions to Help Me Understand My Partner

- Can you say that in a different way?

Things We Wonder About *Flashy Fantastic Rain Forest Frogs*

- I wonder what makes the frogs so colorful.

Read-aloud

In this lesson, the students:

- *Wonder* about a text
- Identify what they learn from the text
- Read independently for up to 30 minutes
- Share their thinking
- Ask clarifying questions

▶1 Review Asking Clarifying Questions

Briefly explain that the students will talk in pairs again today. Refer to the "Questions to Help Me Understand My Partner" chart from Day 1 and explain that you would like them to continue to use the questions when they don't understand their partner's thinking.

▶2 Review the First Reading from *Flashy Fantastic Rain Forest Frogs*

Show the cover of *Flashy Fantastic Rain Forest Frogs* and recall that it is an expository text, a book that gives information about a topic. Refer to the "Things We Wonder About *Flashy Fantastic Rain Forest Frogs*" chart and review that as they heard the first part of the book, the students wondered about rain forest frogs. Ask:

Q *Which ideas on the chart were talked about in the part of the book we read yesterday?*

Have two or three students share which "I wonder" statements on the chart, if any, were talked about in the book. Explain that today they will hear more of the book. The students will again wonder as they listen, and they will listen to find out whether what they wonder about is discussed in the book.

3 Read Aloud with Brief Section Introductions

Remind the students that at the end of the previous reading they learned that some large horned frogs have green and brown bodies that blend with the rain forest floor. Tell the students that the first part of the book you will read today describes how the colors of horned frogs and other frogs help to protect them from predators.

Read pages 10–15 and page 27 aloud, showing the illustrations and stopping as described below.

Suggested Vocabulary

disguise: outward appearance that hides what something really is (p. 10)

predators: animals that live by hunting other animals (p. 12)

glides: moves smoothly and easily (p. 12)

game: animals hunted for food (p. 15)

doses: amounts of a medicine that are given at one time (p. 27)

ELL Vocabulary

English Language Learners may benefit from discussing additional vocabulary, including:

patterns: arrangements of colors (p. 10)

fearlessly: without being afraid (p. 14)

poisonous: capable of harming or killing by poison (p. 14)

Stop after:

> **p. 12**   "When the frog reaches another tree, it can hang on with just one giant toe pad until it can grab with its foot."

Ask:

Q *Based on what you've heard, what are you wondering?*

Use "Turn to Your Partner" to have the students talk about their ideas. After a few minutes, have two or three students share their ideas with the class, and add these ideas to the "Things We Wonder About *Flashy Fantastic Rain Forest Frogs*" chart. Explain that the next part you will read describes an unusual rain forest frog called the poison dart frog. Read pages 14–15 and stop after:

> **p. 15**   "The skin of one small frog can contain enough poison to kill more than a hundred people."

Ask:

Q *Based on what you've heard, what are you wondering?*

Teacher Note ▶

Circulate as partners talk. Notice whether the students are wondering about the text. Also, note whether they are asking clarifying questions when necessary. Be prepared to share your observations with the students at the end of the lesson.

Have the students use "Turn to Your Partner" to discuss their thinking. After a few minutes, have two or three students share with the class. Add these ideas to the chart. Explain that the last part of the book you will read today tells how scientists have found ways to use the poison of the poison dart frog. Read page 27 and stop after:

p. 27 *"Others could be used as heart-attack medicines."*

Follow the procedure you used at the previous stop, including adding the students' "I wonder" statements to the chart.

FACILITATION TIP

During this unit, we invite you to practice **responding neutrally** with interest during class discussions. To respond neutrally means to refrain from overtly praising (e.g., "Great idea" or "Good job") or criticizing (e.g., "That's wrong") the students' responses. Although it may feel more natural to avoid criticism rather than to avoid praise, research shows that both kinds of response encourage students to look to you, rather than to themselves, for validation. To build the students' intrinsic motivation, try responding with genuine curiosity and interest (e.g., "Interesting—say more about that") while avoiding statements that communicate judgment, whether positive or negative.

4▶ Discuss the Reading and "I Wonder" Statements

First in pairs, and then as a class, have the students discuss which of their "I wonder" statements are addressed in the part of the book they heard today. Be ready to reread passages aloud and to show illustrations again to help the students recall what they heard. Ask:

Q *What ideas that you wondered about were discussed in the book?*

Q *What did you learn about how scientists use poison from poison dart frogs?*

Q *What did you learn about how rain forest frogs hide from predators?*

Remind the students that *wondering,* or *questioning,* is an important comprehension strategy because it helps readers think more deeply about a text. Explain that in the next lesson you will finish reading the book and the students will continue to wonder as they listen.

5▶ Discuss Partner Work

Briefly share your observations of how partners worked together. Ask:

Q *How did you show respect for your partner today? What did you do to show respect for your partner's thinking?*

Students might say:

"I was polite when I asked my partner a clarifying question."

"I let my partner finish talking before I talked."

"I listened respectfully to my partner's ideas even when I
  disagreed with her."

Save the "Things We Wonder About *Flashy Fantastic Rain Forest
Frogs*" chart for Day 3.

INDIVIDUALIZED DAILY READING

 ## Document IDR Conferences

Have the students read nonfiction books independently for up to
30 minutes.

Use the "IDR Conference Notes" record sheet to conduct and
document individual conferences.

 At the end of independent reading, have the students discuss their
reading, first in pairs, and then as a class. Ask questions such as:

Q *What is your book about?*

Q *What features of expository text does your book have? What did
you learn from reading the caption that goes with the photograph
of the [elephant's tusks]?*

Guided Strategy Practice

In this lesson, the students:

- *Wonder* about a text read aloud
- Identify what they learn from the text
- Read independently for up to 30 minutes
- Ask clarifying questions

Materials

- *Flashy Fantastic Rain Forest Frogs* (pages 28–31)
- "Things We Wonder About *Flashy Fantastic Rain Forest Frogs*" chart and a marker
- *Student Response Book* pages 44–45
- *Assessment Resource Book*

> Things We Wonder About Flashy Fantastic Rain Forest Frogs
>
> - I wonder what makes the frogs so colorful.

▶1 Review *Flashy Fantastic Rain Forest Frogs*

Have partners sit together. Show the cover of *Flashy Fantastic Rain Forest Frogs* and review that in the previous lesson the students heard more of the book and listened to find out whether what they wondered about rain forest frogs was discussed. Refer to the "Things We Wonder About *Flashy Fantastic Rain Forest Frogs*" chart and ask:

Q *Which questions on the chart have not been talked about in the book so far?*

Explain that today you will read the last few pages of the book aloud. The students will again wonder and listen to find out whether their "I wonder" statements are addressed in the book.

▶2 Read the Last Part of the Book Aloud

Explain that the last part of the book describes how some types of rain forest frogs are becoming extinct (dying out). Then, read pages 28–31 of *Flashy Fantastic Rain Forest Frogs* aloud without stopping. Show the illustrations as you read.

Suggested Vocabulary

threatened: in danger (p. 28)

harvesting wood: cutting down trees to use the wood for lumber, paper, and other products (p. 28)

become extinct: no longer exist; die out (p. 28)

ultraviolet light: light from the sun that is invisible to the human eye; some forms of ultraviolet light are harmful to humans and may also harm animals (p. 31)

 ## Reread and Write "I Wonder" Statements

Have the students turn to *Student Response Book* page 44 and point out that the excerpt is the part of the book you just read aloud. Explain that you would like the students to follow along as you reread the excerpt and that you will read the passage again so they will have another opportunity to think and wonder about it.

Reread the excerpt aloud, without stopping.

Direct the students' attention to *Student Response Book* page 45 "What I Wonder About *Flashy Fantastic Rain Forest Frogs.*" Explain that you would like the partners to talk about what they learned and what they wondered about as they heard and read the excerpt. Each student will then write what she wondered about on page 45. Explain that the students should write their ideas in the form of "I wonder" statements.

 ELL Note

You might want to model writing "I wonder" statements for your English Language Learners.

CLASS COMPREHENSION ASSESSMENT

Circulate as the students work. Ask yourself:

Q *Are the students able to articulate what they learned from the excerpt?*

Q *Are they able to generate "I wonder" statements?*

Record your observations on page 23 of the *Assessment Resource Book.*

Discuss the Reading and the "I Wonder" Statements

Facilitate a whole-class discussion by asking:

Q *What do you wonder about the part of the book we read today?*

> ***Students might say:***
>
> "I wonder what people are doing to protect the rain forest frogs."
>
> "I wonder if the frogs are disappearing in the United States, too."

As volunteers share, add the ideas to the "Things We Wonder About *Flashy Fantastic Rain Forest Frogs*" chart.

Q *What did you learn about why some rain forest frog species are disappearing?*

Q *Do you think it is important to protect frogs that are disappearing? Why or why not?*

Refer to the chart and point out that some ideas the students wondered about are not discussed in the parts of the book they heard. Ask:

Q *How can we find more information about rain forest frogs?*

Explain that in the next lesson the students will practice wondering as they read independently.

Save the "Things We Wonder About *Flashy Fantastic Rain Forest Frogs*" chart for the next lesson. Make *Flashy Fantastic Rain Forest Frogs* available for the students to read independently.

INDIVIDUALIZED DAILY READING

 Read and Wonder

Have the students read nonfiction independently for up to 30 minutes. Explain that at the end of IDR today each student will tell his partner about the book he is reading and what he is still wondering about.

As the students read, circulate among them. Stop and ask individual students to talk about the books they are reading and what they are wondering about. Ask questions such as:

Q *What is your book about?*

Q *What are you still wondering about?*

 At the end of independent reading, have the students share their books and what they are wondering about in pairs.

EXTENSION

Read More About Rain Forests

Continue to explore rain forests with the students by reading aloud one or more of the books listed below. Ask the students to wonder as they listen, and stop periodically to have the students share what they are wondering. Some books you might use are *The Great Kapok Tree: A Tale of the Amazon Rain Forest* by Lynne Cherry, *The Most Beautiful Roof in the World: Exploring the Rainforest Canopy* by Kathryn Lasky, *Rainforest Birds* by Bobbie Kalman, and *A Walk in the Rainforest* by Kristin Joy Pratt.

Day 4

Materials

- "Things We Wonder About *Flashy Fantastic Rain Forest Frogs*" chart
- Expository text for teacher modeling (see Step 2)
- A variety of expository texts at appropriate levels for independent reading
- *Student Response Book* page 46

Independent Strategy Practice

In this lesson, the students:

- *Wonder* about texts read independently
- Ask clarifying questions

 ## Review the Week

Refer to the "Things We Wonder About *Flashy Fantastic Rain Forest Frogs*" chart and remind the students that this week they listened to *Flashy Fantastic Rain Forest Frogs*, learned about rain forest frogs, and talked about what they wondered about them and whether their "I wonder" statements were addressed in the book. Remind them that partners also focused on asking questions when they did not understand each other, as well as showing respect for one another. Ask:

Q *What happens when partners don't show respect for each other's thinking?*

Q *How can you make sure you are treating your partner's thinking respectfully?*

Students might say:

"If a partner puts down my ideas, I won't say anything."

"When partners don't respect each other, they don't want to work together."

"I can ask my partner if I'm listening and being respectful."

 ## Model Wondering Before Reading

Explain that before they begin to read independently today, partners will talk about what they wonder about the topics of their books. Have the students get their independent reading books and their *Student Response Books* and sit in pairs. Have the students turn to *Student Response Book* page 46, "'I Wonder' Statements."

Model wondering before reading by briefly introducing the expository text you selected. Examine the cover of the book and look at several pages, commenting on any text features in the book. Then read the first two or three sentences and wonder aloud about the book's topic. Model writing "I wonder" statements about it.

3 ▶ Practice Wondering Before Reading

Have the students look at their books in the same way, examining the cover and taking note of text features. Have them read the first two or three sentences of the book, or if they are in the middle of a book, have them reread the last two or three sentences they read. Have them write what they are wondering about in their *Student Response Books.*

 When most students are finished writing, have partners share their ideas.

4 ▶ Read Independently and Share with a Partner

Explain that the students will read independently and then partners will talk about whether what they wondered about is addressed in their reading. Have the students read independently for 15–20 minutes.

At the end of the independent reading time, have the students use "Turn to Your Partner" to talk about what they learned and whether their "I wonder" statements were addressed.

Teacher Note

◀ Circulate among pairs. Listen for evidence that they are talking about their "I wonder" statements and what they learned. If the students are having difficulty, prompt them with questions such as:

Q *What was one thing you wondered about? Was that addressed in your reading? How?*

Q *Now that you've read some of the book, what is the topic and what do you wonder about it?*

Listen for whether the students refer to the text as they talk.

5 ▶ Discuss as a Whole Class

Facilitate a whole-class discussion using the questions that follow. Have a few students share their "I wonder" statements. If a student's "I wonder" statement was addressed, have the student read aloud the part of the text about it. Ask questions such as:

Q *What did you wonder before you began reading?*

Q *Was what you wondered about talked about in your reading? Explain.*

Q *What was one interesting thing you learned as you read today?*

Q *What more do you wonder about now that you've read some of the book?*

 Discuss How Partners Worked Together

Facilitate a brief discussion about how the students worked together.

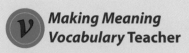 **Making Meaning Vocabulary Teacher**

Next week you will revisit *Flashy Fantastic Rain Forest Frogs* to teach Vocabulary Week 20.

Week 2

Overview

UNIT 7: WONDERING/QUESTIONING
Expository Nonfiction

What Is a Bat?
by Bobbie Kalman and Heather Levigne
(Crabtree, 1999)

This book introduces the reader to the many species of bats and describes bats' characteristics and behavior.

ALTERNATIVE BOOKS

What Is a Fish? by Bobbie Kalman and Allison Larin

Amphibians by Rod Theodorou

Comprehension Focus

- Students use *wondering/questioning* to make sense of nonfiction texts.

- Students *use schema* to make sense of nonfiction texts.

- Students read independently.

Social Development Focus

- Students take responsibility for their learning and behavior.

- Students develop the group skill of asking clarifying questions.

DO AHEAD

- Prepare a chart with the title "Questions About Bats" (for Days 1–3).

- Select an expository book and prepare to model "Stop and Ask Questions" with independent reading on Day 4 (see the Teacher Note on page 372).

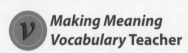

Making Meaning Vocabulary Teacher

If you are teaching Developmental Studies Center's *Making Meaning Vocabulary* program, teach Vocabulary Week 20 this week. For more information, see the *Making Meaning Vocabulary Teacher's Manual.*

Day 1

Materials

- *What Is a Bat?* (pages 3–5 and 12–13)
- *Student Response Book* page 47
- "Questions About Bats" chart, prepared ahead, and a marker
- "Reading Comprehension Strategies" chart

 Note

English Language Learners will benefit from previewing the text and photographs before the read-aloud.

Read-aloud/Strategy Practice

In this lesson, the students:

- Use "Stop and Ask Questions" to think about a text
- Identify what they learn from the text
- Read independently for up to 30 minutes
- Ask clarifying questions

1 Get Ready to Work Together

Gather the class with partners sitting together. Explain that this week the students will continue to focus on asking clarifying questions. Remind the students that practicing this skill helps them work with a partner and builds their reading comprehension skills.

2 Introduce *What Is a Bat?*

Review that in previous lessons the students heard and read expository texts, including articles, functional texts, and books like *Flashy Fantastic Rain Forest Frogs*. Remind them that expository texts give information about a topic. Tell them that this week you will read from another expository text, a book called *What Is a Bat?* Show the cover of the book and read the title. Then turn to the title page and read the authors' names.

Show the table of contents on page 3 and point out that *What Is a Bat?* gives information about bats (for example, what bats look like, where they live, and what they eat).

3 Review "Stop and Ask Questions"

Explain that as you read aloud today the students will write and discuss questions they have about the information in *What Is a Bat?*

Have the students turn to *Student Response Book* page 47, "Stop and Ask Questions About Bats (1)." Remind them that they used "Stop and Ask Questions" in previous lessons during read-alouds and independent reading. Explain that today you will stop four times. At each stop, the students will record their questions in the appropriate box.

 Read Aloud with "Stop and Ask Questions"

Explain that the students will hear two chapters of the book today. The first chapter is titled "What is a bat?" The first part you will read describes characteristics that most bats have in common.

Read pages 4–5 and 12–13 aloud to the class, following the procedure described on the next page.

Suggested Vocabulary

mammals: warm-blooded animals that have a backbone (p. 4)

skillfully: with skill; done well (p. 5)

mate: male or female of a pair of animals (p. 12)

predators: animals that kill and eat other animals (p. 12)

megabats: large bats (p. 12)

dim: somewhat dark; not bright (p. 12)

microbats: small bats (p. 12)

echolocation: an animal's ability to locate objects in its environment by sending out and receiving sounds (p. 12)

agave: a desert plant (p. 13)

baobab trees: trees that produce a type of fruit called monkey fruit and grow in hot areas of the world (p. 13)

ELL Vocabulary

English Language Learners may benefit from discussing additional vocabulary, including:

backbone: series of bones running down the center of the back (p. 4)

patience: ability to put up with trouble or delay without getting upset (p. 5)

avoid: keep away from (p. 5)

ripe: fully grown and ready to be eaten (p. 12)

keen: sharp; highly developed (p. 12)

ELL Note

Consider modeling this for your English Language Learners.

Read page 4, showing the illustrations and reading the captions, and stop after:

> **p. 4**   "Most bats fly at night and rest during the day."

Ask:

Q *What question can you ask right now?*

 Use "Turn to Your Partner" to have the students discuss their questions. Then have the students individually record their questions in the Stop 1 box on page 47 of their *Student Response Books*. After a minute or two, have one or two students share their questions with the class and record the questions on the "Questions About Bats" chart exactly as they are stated.

Explain that the last part of the chapter is called "Difficult to study," and that this part tells why bats are hard for scientists to study. Read page 5 and stop after:

> **p. 5**   "They can easily avoid objects in their path, including traps and nets."

Ask:

Q *What question can you ask right now?*

 Follow the procedure you used at the previous stop. Have the students discuss and record their questions, and then record one or two questions on the chart.

Explain that the second chapter you will read today is titled "Sight and smell," and that it tells how bats use their senses of sight and smell. The first section you will read focuses on bats' sight. Read page 12 and stop after:

> **p. 12**   "Microbats have small eyes, so they rely on echolocation to find food."

 Follow the procedure you used at the previous stop to have the students discuss and record their questions, and then add a few questions to the chart. Explain that the last part of the book you

Teacher Note ▶

If the students have difficulty generating questions at the first stop, model a few and record them on the "Questions About Bats" chart (for example, "How much fur does a bat have on its body?" "How many babies does a bat have at one time?" "Where do bats rest during the day?").

will read today tells about bats' sense of smell. Continue reading pages 12–13 and stop after:

p. 13   "Bats look for plants whose flowers open at night, such as the agave, India trumpet-flower, and baobab trees."

 Follow the procedure you used at the previous stop to have the students discuss and record their questions, and then add a few questions to the chart.

5 ▶ **Discuss the Reading and Questions**

 In pairs, have the students discuss the reading using their questions. Then facilitate a whole-class discussion, using the questions that follow. Be ready to reread passages aloud and show illustrations again to help the students recall what they heard. Ask:

Q   *What is a question that got you and your partner talking? Is that question addressed in the book? How do you know?*

Q   *Do others agree that the question is [addressed in that way/not addressed]? Explain your thinking.*

Students might say:

"My partner asked 'What do bats eat?' The book said some bats eat figs and flowers."

"We disagree with [Hector and Eric] that bats eat flowers. They eat nectar from flowers, but not the petals and the other parts."

"In addition to what [Hector and Eric] said, the book said that vampire bats hunt other animals for food."

If the students do not talk about a bat's eyesight or sense of smell during the discussion, ask:

Q   *What did you learn about a bat's eyesight? About its sense of smell?*

Remind the students that *wondering/questioning* is a comprehension strategy that helps them to think about texts. Explain that tomorrow the students will have another chance to think about their reading using "Stop and Ask Questions" and to work in pairs.

Save the "Questions About Bats" chart for the next lesson.

Teacher Note

You may want to review that most expository texts have features that give readers additional information. Point out that *What Is a Bat?* has some of these features. Show them the table of contents (page 3); the chapter title, drawings, photos, and captions (pages 4–5); "Words to know" (page 31); and the Index (page 32).

INDIVIDUALIZED DAILY READING

 Review the "Reading Comprehension Strategies" Chart

Refer to the "Reading Comprehension Strategies" chart and review the strategies on it. Encourage the students to use these strategies to make sense of their reading.

Have the students read expository books independently for up to 30 minutes.

As the students read, circulate among them and talk to individuals about their reading. Ask questions such as:

Q *What is your book about? What's happening in your book right now?*

Q *What are you wondering about [how rockets work]?*

Q *What strategies are you using to help you understand the reading?*

At the end of independent reading, have the students share what they read as a whole class. Ask questions such as:

Q *What is a reading comprehension strategy on the chart you used when reading today? Where did you use it? How did it help you understand the story?*

EXTENSION

Read More from *What Is a Bat?*

Read "Bat family tree" (page 6) and "A bat's body" (pages 8–9) aloud. As they listen, have the students pay attention to questions that come to mind. After the reading, discuss their questions and what they learned about bats.

Reading Comprehension Strategies

- *visualizing*

 Note

You might want to ask your English Language Learners to think about their answers to these questions as they read independently.

Day 2

Read-aloud/Strategy Practice

Materials

- *What Is a Bat?* (pages 20, 24, and 27)
- *Student Response Book* page 48
- "Questions About Bats" chart from Day 1 and a marker

In this lesson, the students:

- Use "Stop and Ask Questions" to think about a text
- Identify what they learn from the text
- Read independently for up to 30 minutes
- Use prompts to add to one another's thinking
- Ask clarifying questions

 **Review Questioning**

Have partners sit together. Review that in the previous lesson the students heard part of *What Is a Bat?* and used "Stop and Ask Questions" to think about what they heard. Remind them that good readers often ask themselves questions as they read to better understand what they are reading. Ask:

Q *What have you learned so far about bats?*

2 Read Aloud with "Stop and Ask Questions"

Have the students turn to *Student Response Book* page 48, "Stop and Ask Questions About Bats (2)." Explain that today you will read more from *What Is a Bat?* and ask the students to pay attention to the questions that come to mind. You will stop four times. At each stop, the students will talk in pairs about their questions, and then write the questions in the appropriate box on the "Stop and Ask Questions" page.

Read pages 20, 24, and 27 aloud, following the procedure described on the next page.

◀ **Teacher Note**

You may need to reread parts of the book aloud and show illustrations from pages 4–5 and 12–13 to help the students recall what they heard.

Suggested Vocabulary

digest: break down food in the stomach into a form that can be used by the body (p. 20)

fiber: material in a plant that cannot be digested (p. 20)

tropical: having to do with hot, rainy areas of the world known as the tropics (p. 24)

available: possible to get (p. 24)

ELL Vocabulary

English Language Learners may benefit from discussing additional vocabulary, including:

claws: sharp, curved nails on an animal's feet (p. 20)

cling: hold on tightly (p. 27)

Explain that you'll be reading three chapters of the book today. The first chapter is called "Bat food." Read page 20 and stop after:

> **p. 20** "Some bats eat mainly fish." (Note that this sentence is in the middle of a paragraph.)

Ask:

Q *What questions come to mind at this point in the reading?*

 Have the students use "Turn to Your Partner" to discuss their questions. Then have them individually record their questions in the Stop 1 box on page 48 of their *Student Response Books*.

> ***Students might write:***
>
> "How do bats catch so many insects so fast?"
>
> "Who figured out how many bugs a bat can eat in 20 minutes?"
>
> "How do bats catch fish?"

When most students are done, ask one or two volunteers to share their questions with the class. Record the questions on the "Questions About Bats" chart.

Reread the last sentence before the stop, and then read to the end of page 20. Stop after:

> **p. 20** "They spit out the tough fiber and seeds or pass it through their body as waste."

Questions About
Bats

- What do bats eat?

Ask:

Q *What questions come to mind at this point in the reading?*

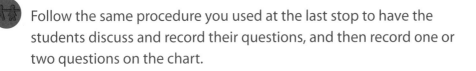 Follow the same procedure you used at the last stop to have the students discuss and record their questions, and then record one or two questions on the chart.

Explain that the next chapter you will read is called "Hey baby!" and that this chapter tells about baby bats. Read page 24 and stop after:

> **p. 24** "Bats that live in places with cold winters have their young in the spring."

As before, have the students discuss and record their questions, and then add a few questions to the chart. Tell the students that the last chapter you will read today is "Growing up" and that the chapter tells more about young bats. Read page 27 and stop after:

> **p. 27** "Once the pup can fly, it can begin to find its own food."

Follow the procedure you used at the previous stops to have the students discuss and record their questions, and then add a few questions to the chart.

3 ▶ Discuss the Reading and Questions

In pairs, have the students use their questions to discuss the reading.

After most pairs are finished talking, facilitate a whole-class discussion. Ask:

Q *What is a question that got you and your partner talking about the reading? How was that question addressed in the book?*

> **Students might say:**
>
> "My partner [Kya] and I asked if bats live mainly in tropical areas. We think the question is answered because the book says bats live in tropical areas where there is food all year round."

Q *Do others agree that the question is [addressed/not addressed]? Refer to the text to support your thinking.*

Teacher Note

Circulate as partners talk. Notice whether the students are generating relevant questions and are referring to the text to decide whether their questions are answered.

Teacher Note

Be ready to reread passages aloud and show illustrations again to help the students recall what they heard.

Students might say:

"We disagree with [Kya and Sue]. The book doesn't say that bats live mainly in hot places. It says that bats live in both hot and cold places."

"I agree with [Tobie and Keith]. In the book, it says that bats in the tropics have babies year-round, but bats in cold climates have them only in the spring. It doesn't really say if there are more bats in hot places."

Teacher Note ▶

Stop early in the discussion and remind the students to use the prompts they know, namely:

- *I agree with _____ because…*

- *I disagree with _____ because…*

- *In addition to what _____ said, I think…*

If the students do not talk about baby bats and what bats eat during the discussion, ask:

Q *What more did you learn today about what bats eat? What did you learn about baby bats?*

Explain that tomorrow the students will learn more about vampire bats and use "Stop and Ask Questions" again to help them think about the reading.

Save the "Questions About Bats" chart for the next lesson.

INDIVIDUALIZED DAILY READING

 Document IDR Conferences

Explain to the students that at the end of independent reading today partners will share one or two things they are learning from their books and something they are still wondering. Remind the students to read with those tasks in mind.

Have the students read nonfiction and expository texts independently for up to 30 minutes.

As the students read, use the "IDR Conference Notes" record sheet to conduct and document individual conferences.

At the end of independent reading, have partners share what they learned and what they are still wondering about what they are reading. Remind the students to ask clarifying questions to help them understand their partners' thinking.

EXTENSION

Distinguish Between Facts and Opinions

Explain to the students that when they read expository or other nonfiction text it is important to recognize when the author is stating facts and when he is stating opinions. Recognizing the difference between facts and opinions helps readers judge the accuracy or truthfulness of what they are reading.

Explain that a *fact* is a statement that can be proved true by observation or by checking a reliable source, such as an encyclopedia. (For example, the statement "Some bats eat fruit" is a fact. It can be proved true by observing bats to see what they eat.) An *opinion* is a statement of what someone thinks, feels, or believes about something. (For example, the statement "Bats are scary" is an opinion. It is a statement of what someone feels or believes to be true, but it cannot be proved true.)

Write the sentences below on a sheet of chart paper. Then have the students use "Think, Pair, Share" to think about and discuss whether each statement is a fact or an opinion.

Fact or Opinion?

- Bats are covered with fur and have a backbone.
- Bats are more interesting than other animals.
- Baby bats are called pups.
- Baby bats are cute.

Day 3

Materials

- *What Is a Bat?* (pages 22–23)
- "Questions About Bats" chart and a marker
- *Student Response Book* page 49
- *Assessment Resource Book*
- *Student Response Book,* IDR Journal section

Teacher Note ▶

You may need to reread parts of the book aloud and show illustrations from pages 20, 24, and 27 to help the students recall what they heard.

Guided Strategy Practice

In this lesson, the students:

- Use *questioning* to think about a text
- Identify what they learn from the text
- Read independently for up to 30 minutes
- Use prompts to add to one another's thinking
- Ask clarifying questions

1 ▶ Review What the Students Learned About Bats

Have pairs sit together. Show the students the cover of *What Is a Bat?* and review that in the previous lesson they heard part of the book, asked questions as they listened, and thought about what new information they were learning. Ask:

Q *What have you learned so far about bats?*

Open the book to pages 22–23 and explain that today you will read the chapter called "Vampire bats" aloud. Refer to the "Questions About Bats" chart and ask if there are unanswered questions about vampire bats on it. Explain that you would like the students to listen for answers to those questions. Also, ask them to pay attention to new questions about vampire bats that come up as they listen.

2 ▶ Read Page 23 of *What Is a Bat?* Aloud

Read page 23 aloud, without stopping. Show the illustrations and read the captions aloud.

ELL Vocabulary

English Language Learners may benefit from discussing the following vocabulary:

mammals: warm-blooded animals that have a backbone (p. 23)

prey: an animal that is hunted by another animal for food (p. 23)

laps: licks (p. 23)

3 ▶ Reread and Write Questions

Have the students turn to the excerpt from *What Is a Bat?* on *Student Response Book* page 49, and point out that this is the part of the book you just read aloud. Ask them to follow along as you reread it. Remind them to listen for answers to any unanswered questions and pay attention to new questions that come to mind.

Reread the excerpt aloud without stopping.

Direct the students' attention to the box at the bottom of page 49. Explain that partners will talk about the questions that came to mind as they listened, and then each student will write their questions in the box.

CLASS COMPREHENSION ASSESSMENT

Circulate as the students work. Ask yourself:

Q *Are the students able to write questions about the excerpt?*

Q *Are their questions relevant to the reading?*

Record your observations on page 24 of the *Assessment Resource Book.*

FACILITATION TIP

Continue to focus on **responding neutrally** with interest during class discussions by refraining from overtly praising or criticizing the students' responses. Instead, build the students' intrinsic motivation by responding with genuine curiosity and interest, for example:

- *Interesting—say more about that.*

- *What you said makes me curious. I wonder…*

- *Your idea is [similar to/different from] what [Lupe] said. How is it [similar/different]?*

 Discuss the Reading and Questions

Facilitate a whole-class discussion about the students' questions. Refer to the "Questions About Bats" chart, and ask:

Q *What questions about vampire bats on the chart are answered in the excerpt?*

Q *What new questions do you have about vampire bats?*

Students might say:

"Do cows and pigs feel it when a bat bites them?"

"How much blood do vampire bats drink?"

"Do vampire bats ever bite people?"

As volunteers share their questions, add the questions to the chart.

If the students do not talk about how vampire bats feed, ask:

Q *What did you learn about how vampire bats feed?*

Refer to the chart and point out that some of the questions about bats have not been answered in the parts of the book you have read aloud. Explain that you will make the book available for independent reading so that interested students can read for answers to their questions and learn more about bats.

Explain that in the next lesson the students will ask questions to help them think about the books they are reading independently, and they will have another opportunity to share their thinking in pairs.

INDIVIDUALIZED DAILY READING

5 **Document IDR Conferences/Have the Students Write About What They Learned and Wonder**

Ask the students to notice what they are learning and wondering as they read.

Have the students independently read nonfiction texts for up to 30 minutes.

Use the "IDR Conference Notes" record sheet to conduct and document individual conferences.

At the end of independent reading, have the students write in their IDR Journals about what they learned and what they are wondering. Have a few volunteers share their writing with the class. Encourage the students to ask one another clarifying questions.

EXTENSION

Read More from *What Is a Bat?*

"Bats in nature" (pages 28–29) describes the important role that bats play in nature and the environmental threats and natural enemies that bats face. Read these pages aloud to the students. Use "Stop and Ask Questions" to help the students think about the chapter as they listen. (If you wish, stop at the end of each subsection and have the students jot down their questions in their IDR Journals.) After the reading, discuss the students' questions and add them to the chart.

Day 4

Independent Strategy Practice

Materials

- Expository text for teacher modeling (see Step 3)
- A variety of expository texts at appropriate levels for independent reading
- Small self-stick notes for each student

In this lesson, the students:

- Use "Stop and Ask Questions" to think about texts they read independently
- Identify what they learn from the text

1 Review the Week

Have partners sit together. Review that this week the students heard parts of *What Is a Bat?* and used "Stop and Ask Questions" to help them make sense of the reading. Remind them that they also considered whether their questions were answered.

2 Review "Stop and Ask Questions" with Independent Reading

Explain that the students will use "Stop and Ask Questions" as they read independently today. They will use self-stick notes to mark any place in their reading where a question comes to mind and they will jot their questions on the notes. Remind them that they used self-stick notes in this way earlier in the year to ask questions about stories they were reading independently. Review that the purpose for asking questions is to help them think about the text. Explain that they will use the questions later to discuss their reading.

Teacher Note

Have the question you will ask in mind ahead of time so this modeling goes smoothly. (For example, you might say, "The book says that spring is tornado time. That means that tornadoes usually strike in warm weather. I wonder why that is? I'm going to write down the question, 'Why are tornadoes more common in the spring?' and stick it here next to this paragraph about tornado time.")

3 Model "Stop and Ask Questions" with Independent Reading

Model the procedure by briefly introducing the expository text you selected. Read several sentences, and think aloud about a question, jot the question on a self-stick note, and place the note in the margin where you stopped reading.

Explain that partners will share their questions and discuss whether the questions are answered in their books.

4 ▶ Read Independently

Have the students read independently for 15–20 minutes. Stop the class at 5-minute intervals to have partners share any questions they have written so far.

◀ **Teacher Note**

At the first stop, remind partners to tell one another what their books are about and what they just read.

5 ▶ Discuss the Students' Questions

At the end of the independent reading time, have the students use "Turn to Your Partner" to talk about their questions and whether the questions are answered. Remind the students to explain their thinking by referring to the text.

Have a few volunteers share their questions with the class. Ask the students to report what they were reading about when the question came to mind and to state the question. Probe the students' thinking by asking:

Q *What was happening in the book when that question came to mind?*

Q *How would you answer that question right now? What evidence in the book makes you think that?*

Explain that the students will have more opportunities to use "Stop and Ask Questions" to think about and discuss their independent reading. Emphasize that although the students will not always be expected to write down their questions, they will be expected to think of questions and look for answers whenever they read.

◀ **Teacher Note**

Circulate among pairs. Listen for evidence that the students asked questions during their reading and are referring to the texts to determine whether their questions are answered. If the students are not using the texts to support their conclusions, note this and focus on it during your instruction next week. In addition, you can ask questions such as:

Q *Where in the text is that answered?*

Q *How does that answer your question?*

6 ▶ Reflect on Working Together

Review that this week the students focused on asking clarifying questions. Have the students use "Think, Pair, Share" to talk about questions such as:

Q *Think about how you and your partner worked together this week. How has your ability to share your thinking improved? How has that helped your work together?*

Q *How do you think you and your partner are doing with asking each other clarifying questions? How has this helped your learning?*

Q *What is one way you are learning to take responsibility for your own thinking and behavior?*

EXTENSION

Practice in Content Area Reading

Have the students use "Stop and Ask Questions" in social studies, science, math, or other content area reading. Encourage them to use self-stick notes to mark places where questions arise and to look for answers to their questions.

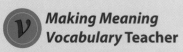

**Making Meaning
Vocabulary Teacher**

Next week you will revisit
What Is a Bat? to teach
Vocabulary Week 21.

Week 3   Overview

UNIT 7: WONDERING/QUESTIONING
Expository Nonfiction

"Why Do Animals Play?"
by Kathleen Weidner Zoehfeld
(Carus Publishing, 2007)

This article explores the role of play in the life of young animals.

"Feeling the Heat"
by Kathryn R. Satterfield
(timeforkids.com, 2007)

The effects of global warming on polar bears is explained in this article.

"Banning Tag"

This article outlines the current trend in schools across the country to ban the game of tag at recess.

ALTERNATIVE RESOURCES

National Geographic Explorer,
magma.nationalgeographic.com/ngexplorer/articles

Science News for Kids,
sciencenewsforkids.org

Comprehension Focus

• Students identify what they learn from articles.

• Students use *wondering/questioning* to make sense of nonfiction articles.

• Students *use schema* to make sense of nonfiction articles.

• Students read independently.

Social Development Focus

• Students take responsibility for their learning and behavior.

• Students develop the group skill of asking clarifying questions.

DO AHEAD

• Prepare a chart with the title "Questions About 'Why Do Animals Play?'" (for Day 1).

• Prepare a chart with the title "Questions About 'Feeling the Heat'" (for Day 2).

• Prepare a chart with the title "Questions About 'Banning Tag'" (for Day 3).

• Make copies of the Unit 7 Parent Letter (BLM21) to send home with the students on the last day of the unit.

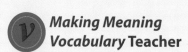

Making Meaning Vocabulary Teacher

If you are teaching Developmental Studies Center's *Making Meaning Vocabulary* program, teach Vocabulary Week 21 this week. For more information, see the *Making Meaning Vocabulary Teacher's Manual*.

Day 1

Materials

- "Why Do Animals Play?" (see pages 383–384)

- "Questions to Help Me Understand My Partner" chart (from Week 1)

- "Questions About 'Why Do Animals Play?'" chart, prepared ahead

- "Self-monitoring Questions" chart

Questions/Statements to Help Me Understand My Partner

- *I'm not sure I understand you.*

- *What did you mean when you said…?*

Read-aloud/Strategy Practice

In this lesson, the students:

- Use "Stop and Ask Questions" to think about an article

- Identify what they learn from an article

- Read independently for up to 30 minutes

- Ask clarifying questions

▶ 1 Get Ready to Work Together

Have partners sit together. Review that in previous lessons the students heard and read expository texts, including articles, functional texts, and books like *What Is a Bat?* and *Flashy Fantastic Rain Forest Frogs.* Remind them that expository texts give information about a topic. Tell them that this week you will read several articles and the students will use the comprehension strategy of *questioning* to help them make sense of the articles.

Refer to the "Questions to Help Me Understand My Partner" chart, and remind the students that partners have been asking each other clarifying questions. Explain that this week the students will continue to focus on asking clarifying questions. Ask and briefly discuss:

Q *What clarifying questions have you asked your partner to help you understand your partner's thinking?*

Q *How did you ask those questions in a caring and respectful way?*

Q *Why is it important for you to understand your partner's thinking?*

Introduce "Why Do Animals Play?"

Read aloud the title of the article and the author's name to the students. Explain that this article is from a magazine for children. Tell the students that you will stop as you read aloud today and they will share and discuss questions they have about the information in "Why Do Animals Play?" Remind them that they used "Stop and Ask Questions" in previous lessons during read-alouds and in their independent reading. Explain that today you will stop four times as you read. At each stop, the students will share their questions in pairs and with the class.

ELL Note

English Language Learners will benefit from previewing the article prior to the read-aloud. Stop frequently to check for the students' understanding.

 Read Aloud with "Stop and Ask Questions"

Read the text of the article aloud, showing the illustrations and stopping as described below.

Suggested Vocabulary

frolic: play (p. 383)

fawn: young deer (p. 383)

predators: animals that kill and eat other animals (p. 383)

stalks: follows and sneaks up on (p. 383)

ELL Vocabulary

English Language Learners may benefit from discussing additional vocabulary, including:

pounce: move very quickly and suddenly onto something (p. 383)

leap: jump (p. 383)

survival: ability to stay alive (p. 383)

crouched legs: bent legs, close to the ground waiting to run forward (p. 383)

curious: interested in things (p. 383)

frisky: playful (p. 384)

snout: nose (p. 384)

keep their footing: not fall over (p. 384)

straying youngsters: young animals moving away from the group (p. 384)

 ELL Note

Help your English Language Learners understand words such as *pounce*, *leap*, and *crouched* by briefly acting out the words. Then after the read-aloud, review the words with your students, have the students say the words, and act them out.

Read the first several sentences and stop after:

p. 383 "But there is more to animal play than just fun."

Ask:

Q *What question can you ask right now?*

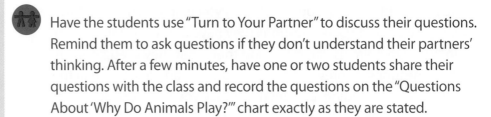 Have the students use "Turn to Your Partner" to discuss their questions. Remind them to ask questions if they don't understand their partners' thinking. After a few minutes, have one or two students share their questions with the class and record the questions on the "Questions About 'Why Do Animals Play?'" chart exactly as they are stated.

Continue reading, and stop after:

> **p. 383** "While deer have to learn to escape from predators, young lion cubs must learn how to hunt."

Again ask:

Q *What question can you ask right now?*

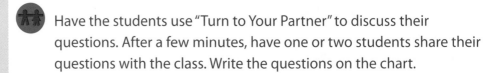 Have the students use "Turn to Your Partner" to discuss their questions. After a few minutes, have one or two students share their questions with the class. Write the questions on the chart.

Reread the last sentence before the stop, and continue reading. Follow the procedure you used at the previous stops, adding a few of the student questions to the chart. Stop after:

> **p. 383** "So, they must learn to communicate."

> **p. 384** "If one youngster plays too rough, the others will let him know they are unhappy with his behavior."

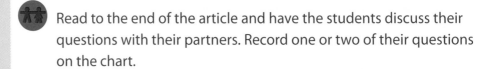 Read to the end of the article and have the students discuss their questions with their partners. Record one or two of their questions on the chart.

4 ▶ **Discuss the Reading and Questions**

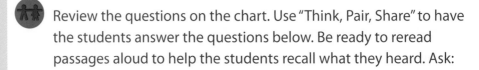 Review the questions on the chart. Use "Think, Pair, Share" to have the students answer the questions below. Be ready to reread passages aloud to help the students recall what they heard. Ask:

Q *What questions on the chart are answered in the article?*

Q *Do others agree that the question is [answered/not answered] in the article? Explain your thinking.*

Q *What did you learn about why animals play?*

Q *Think back to when you were younger. What did you learn from playing?*

Students might say:

"My partner and I think that the question 'How do wolf pups communicate?' is answered in the article. It says that the pups signal each other that they want to play by stretching out their front legs and bowing."

"In addition to what [Hector] said, the wolf pups also hold their mouths open and wag their tails to let the other pups know they are playing."

"Animals play so they can learn how to act as adult animals. I think when I was real young and I played games with my big sister, I had to learn how to take turns. I think that helped me know how to share and play games with other kids right now."

Remind the students that *questioning* is a comprehension strategy that helps them to think about what they are reading. Explain that tomorrow the students will have another chance to think about their reading using "Stop and Ask Questions" and to work in pairs.

INDIVIDUALIZED DAILY READING

 Review and Practice Self-monitoring with Articles and Other Expository Nonfiction Books

Refer to the "Self-monitoring Questions" chart and review the questions. Remind the students that it is important to stop to think about what they are reading and use the questions to help them track whether they are understanding their reading. When they do not understand, they may need to reread, use a comprehension strategy, or get a different text.

Have the students read articles and other expository texts at their appropriate reading levels independently for up to 30 minutes. Stop them at 10-minute intervals and have them monitor their comprehension by thinking about the questions on the chart.

Self-monitoring Questions

- What is happening in my story right now?

- Does the reading make sense?

Circulate among the students and ask individual students to read a passage to you and tell you what it is about.

At the end of the reading time, have a whole-class discussion about how the students used the self-monitoring questions to track their reading comprehension. Ask questions such as:

Q *Which self-monitoring question did you find the most helpful? Why?*

Q *What do you want to continue to be aware of when you read to make sure you understand what you are reading?*

Why Do Animals Play?

by Kathleen Weidner Zoehfeld

from *ASK Magazine* (May/June 2007)

Puppies love to run and tumble. They chase each other around the yard. They wrestle and nip each other gently. A kitten will pounce on a toy mouse or leap high for a piece of yarn. Why do animals play? For the same reason YOU play—because it's FUN! But there is more to animal play than just fun. For animals in the wild, play is important to their very survival. Young animals have to learn about their world. They have to exercise their muscles and practice all the skills they will need to be successful adults.

Sometimes a young deer will leap and frolic. With each twisting, twirling dance, the fawn's legs are getting stronger. It is learning how to run fast and zigzag to confuse predators. That will keep it safe when it is time to leave its mother's side.

While deer have to learn to escape from predators, young lion cubs must learn how to hunt. When a cub is little, it stalks its brother or sister. It will slink along on crouched legs. When the moment seems right, the cub pounces! The other cub bats back with its paws and wriggles free.

The cubs keep their claws in, though, and their bites are gentle. The cubs are not trying to hurt each other. They are playing at being great hunters. This is practice for the real thing.

Wolves live in family groups called packs. When the pups are grown up, they will hunt together and watch out for each other. So, they must learn to communicate.

A wolf pup signals another pup that she wants to play. She stretches out her front legs and bows. She wiggles and wags her tail. As they play, both pups hold their mouths slightly open. That's how they tell each other "yes, we are still playing!"

Much like human children, young dolphins love to play with toys. Wild dolphins are very curious. They explore their world,

continues

Why Do Animals Play?
continued

looking for interesting items. A piece of seaweed might inspire a game. The frisky calves will chase one another, passing the seaweed from snout, to flipper, to tail.

When most young animals wrestle, race, or chase, it's not about winning. Each youngster is building its strength and skills. And they are learning to cooperate. If one youngster plays too rough, the others will let him know they are unhappy with his behavior.

Even when everyone cooperates, play can get dangerous. But animals play anyway! Young mountain goats live all their lives on steep slopes. The kids bump each other and butt heads in fun. If they're not careful, kids can fall and hurt their legs or even break their bones. When they play, the young animals learn to keep their footing no matter what might happen.

Groups of young vervet monkeys sometimes sneak away from the adults in their family. All wrapped up in their games, the little ones may not notice when danger is near. So an adult monkey will go looking for the straying youngsters. The adult will yell out a warning.

Watch out! Be careful! You've heard parents or teachers say these things when you play. Animals have to learn about the dangers in their world too. Playing helps them learn. Playing helps them get along. Playing makes them strong and confident.

Read-aloud/Strategy Practice

In this lesson, the students:

- Use "Stop and Ask Questions" to think about an article
- Identify what they learn from the article
- Read independently for up to 30 minutes
- Ask clarifying questions

1 Get Ready to Work Together

Have partners sit together. Explain that today the students will continue to focus on asking clarifying questions. Remind the students that practicing this skill will help them work in pairs and build their reading comprehension skills.

2 Introduce "Feeling the Heat"

Remind the students that in the previous lesson they heard and discussed the article "Why Do Animals Play?" Explain that today they will hear and read another article and discuss in pairs questions that they have about the article.

Have the students turn to their copy of the article "Feeling the Heat" on *Student Response Book* page 50. Read the title of the article aloud and explain that it was published in January 2007 by timeforkids.com, an online magazine for children. Explain that the article is about polar bears. Tell the students that polar bears can be found in the Arctic Circle. Show the students the picture of the polar bears and the map of the Arctic Circle and point out Alaska and the countries located in the Arctic Circle. Read the information about polar bears in "The Bear Facts" at the end of the article and ask:

Q *What questions do you have about polar bears before hearing the article?*

Materials

- "Feeling the Heat" (see pages 391–392)
- *Student Response Book* pages 50–53
- "Questions About 'Feeling the Heat'" chart, prepared ahead, and a marker
- *Assessment Resource Book*
- "Self-monitoring Questions" chart

 Note

Prior to reading the article aloud, summarize the article. Then read the article aloud to your English Language Learners, stopping frequently to check for understanding. If necessary, reread sections of the article and discuss them with your students.

Call on a few volunteers and list their questions on the "Questions About 'Feeling the Heat'" chart. Tell the students to listen to see if the article answers any of their questions.

 Review "Stop and Ask Questions"

Explain that as you read aloud today the students will write and discuss questions they have about the information in "Feeling the Heat."

Have the students turn to *Student Response Book* page 53, "Stop and Ask Questions About 'Feeling the Heat.'" Explain that today you will stop three times. At each stop, the students will record their questions in the appropriate box.

 Read Aloud with "Stop and Ask Questions"

Read the article, stopping as described below.

Suggested Vocabulary

threatened species: whole group of animals that could completely die out (p. 391)

ultimate survivors: live on until the end (p. 392)

ELL Vocabulary

English Language Learners may benefit from discussing additional vocabulary, including:

harsh conditions: hard life, including living in extremely cold weather (p. 391)

shrinking: getting smaller (p. 391)

scientists: people who study science (p. 391)

air pollution: harmful gases in the air (p. 391)

Stop after:

p. 391 "Studies show that polar ice is shrinking."

Ask:

Q *What question can you ask right now?*

Teacher Note

If the students have difficulty generating questions at the first stop, model a few and record them on the "Questions About 'Feeling the Heat'" chart (for example, "Why is the polar bears' world melting?" "What's making the ice shrink?" "Do polar bears live anywhere else besides the Arctic Circle?").

Use "Turn to Your Partner" to have the students discuss their questions. Then have the students individually record their questions in the Stop 1 box on page 53 of their *Student Response Books*. After a minute or two, have one or two students share their questions with the class and record the questions on the "Questions About 'Feeling the Heat'" chart.

Reread the last sentence before the stop, and then continue reading. Stop after:

> **p. 392** "But in a warmer world, this process speeds up."

Ask:

Q *What question can you ask right now?*

 Follow the procedure you used at the previous stop. Have the students discuss and record their questions, and then record one or two questions on the chart.

Reread the last sentence before the stop, and then continue reading to the end of the article.

 Follow the procedure you used at the previous stop to have the students discuss and record their questions, and then add a few questions to the chart.

5 ▶ Reread the Article and Discuss

 Have the students turn back to their copy of the article "Feeling the Heat" on *Student Response Book* page 50. In pairs, have the students reread the article and discuss it using their questions. Then facilitate a whole-class discussion using the questions that follow. Be ready to reread passages aloud to help the students recall what they heard.

Ask:

Q *Which of your questions were answered in the article?*

Q *Do others agree that the question is [answered/not answered] in the article? Explain your thinking.*

Q *What did you learn about the effects of global warming on polar bears?*

CLASS COMPREHENSION ASSESSMENT

Circulate as partners work. Randomly select students to observe and ask yourself:

Q *Are the students able to ask questions about what they hear and read?*

Q *Are the students able to make sense of expository nonfiction articles?*

Record your observations on page 25 of the *Assessment Resource Book*.

Explain to the students that after reading articles, readers often have additional questions. Ask:

Q *What additional questions do you have about polar bears and global warming?*

> **Students might say:**
>
> "What rules might the government make to protect the polar bears?"
>
> "Can we save all the polar bears and put them in zoos?"
>
> "What happens if all of the ice in the Arctic Circle melts?"

List several of the students' questions on the chart, and suggest that the students might want to read more about the topic at a later time.

Teacher Note

Save the "Questions About 'Feeling the Heat'" chart for later use (see the Extension on page 390).

 Reflect on Partner Work

Ask and briefly discuss questions such as:

Q *If you didn't understand your partner's thinking what did you do?*

Q *How did you take responsibility for your own learning when you worked with your partner today?*

Q *What can you do to be more responsible the next time you work with your partner?*

INDIVIDUALIZED DAILY READING

 Practice Self-monitoring

Continue to have the students monitor their comprehension. Refer to the "Self-monitoring Questions" chart and review the questions. Ask and briefly discuss:

Q *Which of these questions have you found the most helpful when you are reading?*

Q *What do you want to continue to think about when you are reading independently today?*

Remind the students that it is important to stop to think about what they are reading and to use the questions on the chart to help them track whether they are understanding their reading. When they do not understand what they are reading, they may need to reread, use a comprehension strategy, or get a different text.

Have the students independently read articles and other expository texts at their appropriate reading levels for up to 30 minutes. Stop them at 10-minute intervals and have them monitor their comprehension by thinking about the questions on the chart.

Circulate among the students and ask individual students to read a passage to you, tell you what it is about, and tell you which questions they are using to help them monitor their comprehension.

At the end of the reading time, have a whole-class discussion about how the students used the self-monitoring questions to track their reading comprehension.

> ### Self-monitoring Questions
>
> - What is happening in my story right now?
> - Does the reading make sense?

EXTENSION

Read More About the Effects of Global Warming on Polar Bears

Refer to the "Questions About 'Feeling the Heat'" chart and have the students use "Think, Pair, Share" to choose one or two questions they would like to answer. Have partners search for information on the Internet, in children's magazines, and in the library. Then have the students share with the class the information they found.

Feeling the Heat

by Kathryn R. Satterfield

from timeforkids.com (2007)

Polar bears live on sea ice above the Arctic Circle. About 20,000 polar bears can be found on Earth. Nearly 5,000 live in Alaskan waters.

Nature has prepared them for harsh conditions. But nothing could prepare them for a new danger that they face.

The polar bears' world is melting. Studies show that polar ice is shrinking. Scientists blame global warming. They say that certain kinds of air pollution are quickly making the world too warm.

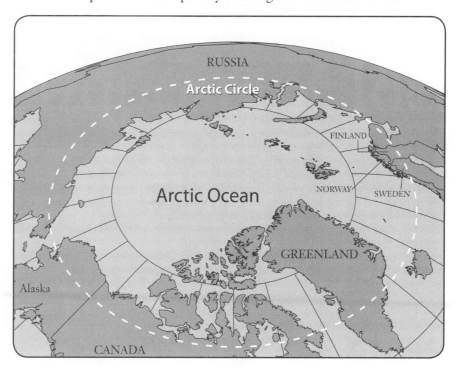

A Big Bear Problem

Two weeks ago, the U.S. government said it was taking steps to list the polar bear as a threatened species. That would help protect the bears.

Polar bears depend on sea ice for their survival. The ice is where they hunt seals, their main source of food.

continues

"Feeling the Heat"

continued

Some melting and refreezing of polar ice is natural. But in a warmer world, this process speeds up. The bears have less time to hunt for food. Many have been found in poor health. The number of bears is falling.

If the government decides to list the bears as threatened, it will make a plan and strict rules to protect them. "Polar bears are nature's ultimate survivors," says Dirk Kempthorne, a lawmaker involved in the decision. With help from humans, these special creatures can bounce back.

The Bear Facts

Big   Male bears can grow to be 11 feet tall. Some weigh as much as 1,400 pounds.

Tough   The bear is built for Arctic temperatures. Two layers of fur keep it warm.

King of the ice   The polar bear has no natural predators.

Day 3

Read-aloud/Strategy Practice

In this lesson, the students:

- Use "Stop and Ask Questions" to think about an article
- Identify what they learn from the article
- Read independently for up to 30 minutes
- Ask clarifying questions

1 Introduce "Banning Tag"

Have partners sit together. Remind the students that they have been asking questions as they read to help them make sense of text, and asking their partners clarifying questions if they don't understand their partners' thinking. Explain that today they will read another article and continue to ask their partners clarifying questions when necessary.

Explain that the article the students will hear today is titled "Banning Tag." Have them turn to *Student Response Book* pages 54–55 and explain that this is a copy of the article. Draw their attention to the article title and section headings and point out that they are in bold print so readers can find them easily. Remind the students that the title and headings are text features that help readers know what information might be in an article.

Have the students follow along in their *Student Response Books* as you read the title and section headings aloud; then ask and briefly discuss:

Q *After reading the title and section headings, what do you think you might learn from this article?*

Have a few volunteers share their thinking.

Materials

- "Banning Tag" (see pages 398–399)
- *Student Response Book* pages 54–56
- "Questions About 'Banning Tag'" chart, prepared ahead, and a marker
- Small self-stick notes for the students

Explain Asking Questions Before Reading

Explain that asking questions before reading can help readers focus on what they are reading. Explain that before the students read today, partners will talk about what questions they have about the article "Banning Tag."

Have the students use "Turn to Your Partner" to discuss questions they have about the article. Then ask them to write two of their questions on *Student Response Book* page 56.

After a few minutes, have several students share their questions with the class. Record the questions on the "Questions About 'Banning Tag'" chart.

Read "Banning Tag" Aloud

Explain to the students that you will read the article aloud without stopping. Then the students will reread the article in pairs and decide if any of their questions are answered in the article. Ask the students to follow along as you read the article aloud.

Read the article aloud, stopping to define the following vocabulary words:

> **Suggested Vocabulary**
>
> **petition:** letter signed by many people asking for something to change or for an action to be taken (p. 399)
>
> **versions:** kinds (p. 399)

Partners Reread "Banning Tag" and Answer Their Questions

Ask partners to review the questions they wrote in their *Student Response Books* prior to hearing the article "Banning Tag" and the questions listed on the "Questions About 'Banning Tag'" chart. Then reread the article together, having partners use self-stick notes to mark places in the article where they think their questions are answered. Tell the students to be ready to share their thinking with the whole class.

5 ▶ Discuss as a Whole Class

Signal for the students' attention and facilitate a whole-class discussion. Ask questions such as:

Q *What questions did you and your partner ask before you heard the article "Banning Tag"?*

Q *Which questions were answered in the article? Where in the article is that question answered? Explain your thinking?*

Q *Which questions were not answered in the article? Explain your thinking.*

Q *What questions do you have for [Paula and Shaq] about their thinking?*

6 ▶ Discuss How Partners Worked Together

Facilitate a brief discussion about how the students worked together. Ask:

Q *What clarifying questions did you ask your partner to help you understand [her] thinking?*

Q *What did you do to take responsibility for your learning and behavior today?*

Explain that in the next lesson the students will ask questions to help them think about the books they are reading independently and they will have another opportunity to share their thinking in pairs.

INDIVIDUALIZED DAILY READING

7 ▶ Have the Students Read for Information/ Document IDR Conferences

Remind the students that one of the purposes of reading expository nonfiction is to learn information about a topic. Explain to the students that today they will read articles and other expository nonfiction independently and will put self-stick notes beside

FACILITATION TIP

Reflect on your experience over the past three weeks with **responding neutrally** with interest during class discussions. Does this practice feel natural to you? Are you integrating it into class discussions throughout the day? What effect is it having on the students? You will have more opportunities to practice this facilitation technique in the next unit.

 Note

Consider modeling this activity for your English Language Learners.

interesting facts and information they are learning. At the end of IDR they will share in pairs some of the facts they have learned.

Distribute self-stick notes to the students and have them read independently for up to 30 minutes. Circulate among the students and ask individual students to read a passage to you and tell you what it is about. Use the "IDR Conference Notes" record sheet to conduct and document individual conferences.

 At the end of IDR have partners review the facts that they noted and choose four of the most interesting facts to share with one another. Have each student share what her article or text is about and the four interesting facts she learned from it.

Banning TAG

Imagine that you are being chased. You run as fast as you can, but you are not quick enough. You feel hands on your back, touching you. You trip, fall down, skinning your knee. Not again! You are tired of always being "it."

Has this ever happened to you? If it has, you know that it does not feel very good. Some principals, teachers, and parents are worried that playing tag at recess is too dangerous. They argue that kids run into one another, fall down, and get hurt playing tag. They say that sometimes tag leads to hitting, pushing, and bullying. In response to these concerns, schools all over the country are banning the game of tag during recess.

The Other Side

Some parents and kids think schools should not ban tag. A third grader from the state of Washington even started a petition to get his principal to change the ban and let the kids play tag again at recess. There are a lot of good things about the game. It is easy to get started, because you do not need anything to play except some friends. Also, while you run around, you are getting exercise and having fun at the same time. Many people are upset that recess has to be ruined for everyone just because a few children play too rough. After all, the game of tag has been around for hundreds of years.

Different Types of Tag

There are many different versions of tag. You probably know how to play different versions. One of the most popular versions of tag is "freeze tag," where instead of being "it" when you are caught, you have to stand still until another player touches you. There is also "tunnel tag," which is like freeze tag, except that your teammate must crawl through your legs before you can play again.

"Monster tag" starts with one person chasing all the others. As each player is tagged, he or she joins hands with "it" to help chase the others.

In the end, there is a long chain of players who are all "it," working together. With all the hands and feet, the chain reminds some people of a monster! That is how this kind of tag got its name.

Other Games

If your school does not allow tag at recess, there are lots of other games you can play instead! If you have a ball, you can organize a game of kick-ball or four-square. With a piece of chalk and a few pebbles, you can play hopscotch. You can probably think of many more fun things to do during recess.

Whatever you are allowed to do at recess, it is important that you play fair and are gentle with others. When everyone feels safe, everyone can have fun!

Day 4

Materials

- A variety of expository texts at appropriate levels for independent reading
- *Assessment Resource Book*
- Unit 7 Parent Letter (BLM21)

Independent Strategy Practice

In this lesson, the students:

- Use "Stop and Ask Questions" to think about texts they read independently
- Identify what they learn from the text
- Ask clarifying questions

1 Review the Week

Have partners sit together. Review that this week the students heard three articles and used "Stop and Ask Questions" to help them make sense of the reading. Remind them that they also considered whether their questions were answered.

2 Review "Stop and Ask Questions" with Independent Reading

Explain that the students will use "Stop and Ask Questions" as they read independently today. Review that the purpose for asking questions is to help them think about the text, and explain that they will use the questions later to discuss their reading.

Explain that the students will read articles and other nonfiction texts. Tell them that you will stop them periodically to think about any questions they have about what they are reading. Explain that partners will then share their questions and discuss whether the questions are answered in their books or articles.

Teacher Note

At the first stop, remind partners to tell each other what their books are about and what they just read.

Circulate among pairs. Listen for evidence that the students asked questions during their reading and are referring to the texts to determine whether their questions are answered.

3 Read Independently

Have the students independently read expository texts for 20 minutes. Stop the class at 5-minute intervals to have partners share any questions they have so far.

Discuss the Students' Questions

At the end of the independent reading, have a few volunteers share their questions with the class. Ask each student to report what he was reading about when the question came to mind and to state the question. Remind the students to explain their thinking by referring to the text.

Probe the students' thinking by asking:

Q *What in the text made you think of that question?*

Q *How would you answer that question right now? What evidence in the text makes you think that?*

Encourage the students to think of questions and look for answers whenever they read.

5 **Reflect on Working Together**

Review that this week the students focused on asking clarifying questions. As a class, discuss questions such as:

Q *Think about how you and your partner worked together this week. How has asking your partner clarifying questions helped you to understand your partner's thinking? How has that helped you learn?*

Q *Why is it important to listen carefully to what others say?*

Q *How have you become more responsible for your own thinking and behavior?*

Teacher Note

This is the last week of Unit 7. You will reassign partners for Unit 8.

INDIVIDUAL COMPREHENSION ASSESSMENT

Before continuing with Unit 8, take this opportunity to assess individual students' progress in thinking about what they are learning and using *wondering/questioning* to help them understand nonfiction text. Please refer to pages 40–41 in the *Assessment Resource Book* for instructions.

SOCIAL SKILLS ASSESSMENT

Take this opportunity to assess your students' social development using the Social Skills Assessment record sheet on pages 2–3 of the *Assessment Resource Book*.

EXTENSION

Continue to Practice Asking Questions in Content-area Reading

Continue to have the students use "Stop and Ask Questions" in social studies, science, math, or other content-area reading. Encourage them to use self-stick notes to mark places where questions arise and to look for answers to their questions. Periodically, have a whole-class discussion about the questions that the students are asking as they read and whether or not the questions are answered in their text.

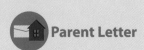

Parent Letter

Send home with each student the Parent Letter for this unit (see "Do Ahead," page 377). Periodically, have a few students share with the class what they are reading at home.

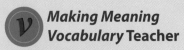

***Making Meaning Vocabulary* Teacher**

Next week you will revisit "Why Do Animals Play?" and "Feeling the Heat" to teach Vocabulary Week 22.

Unit 8

Determining Important Ideas

FICTION AND EXPOSITORY NONFICTION

During this unit, the students make inferences, visualize to understand and enjoy stories, and explore important ideas. During IDR, they think and write about the important ideas in their independent reading books. Socially, they learn and practice the cooperative strategy "Think, Pair, Write." The students also continue to develop the group skills of giving reasons for their ideas and asking clarifying questions. They continue to take responsibility for their learning and behavior and relate the value of respect to their behavior.

Week 1 *Fables* by Arnold Lobel

Week 2 *Lifetimes* by David L. Rice
A Day's Work by Eve Bunting

Week 3 *Keepers* by Jeri Hanel Watts

Week 1

Overview

UNIT 8: DETERMINING IMPORTANT IDEAS

Fiction and Expository Nonfiction

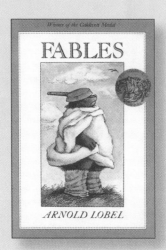

Fables

by Arnold Lobel

(HarperTrophy, 1980)

This book is a collection of fables. The fables that will be used are "The Camel Dances," "The Mouse at the Seashore," and "The Young Rooster."

ALTERNATIVE BOOKS

Tico and the Golden Wings by Leo Lionni

The Gold Coin by Alma Flor Ada

Comprehension Focus

- Students *explore important ideas* in stories.

- Students *make inferences* to understand stories.

- Students *visualize* to understand and enjoy stories.

- Students *synthesize* by interpreting a story's message or theme.

- Students read independently.

Social Development Focus

- Students take responsibility for their learning and behavior.

- Students develop the group skill of giving reasons for their ideas.

- Students learn and practice the cooperative structure "Think, Pair, Write."

- Students participate in a check-in class meeting.

DO AHEAD

- Prior to Day 1, decide how you will randomly assign partners to work together during the unit.

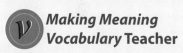

Making Meaning Vocabulary Teacher

If you are teaching Developmental Studies Center's *Making Meaning Vocabulary* program, teach Vocabulary Week 22 this week. For more information, see the *Making Meaning Vocabulary Teacher's Manual*.

Day 1

Materials

- "The Camel Dances" in *Fables* (pages 22–23)
- "Reading Comprehension Strategies" chart
- Small self-stick notes for each student

Read-aloud/Strategy Lesson

In this lesson, the students:

- *Visualize* a story
- *Explore important ideas* in the story
- Connect important ideas to their own lives
- Read independently for up to 30 minutes
- Explain their thinking

About Exploring Important Ideas

The focus in this unit is on *exploring important ideas,* a powerful strategy for helping readers understand and retain what they read. In the *Making Meaning* program, the focus is on helping the students identify the important ideas in stories and articles rather than identifying one "main idea." The students identify what they feel are the important ideas and support their opinions with evidence from the text. The students informally synthesize their thinking about the text by interpreting its important messages or themes. (For further discussion about determining important ideas, please see volume 1, page xvi.)

 Pair Students and Get Ready to Work Together

Randomly assign partners and have them sit together. Explain that the same pairs will work together for the next few weeks and that they will focus on explaining their thinking more clearly by giving reasons for their ideas.

2 Introduce *Fables*

Explain to the students that this week they will be reading a kind of story called a fable.

Explain that fables are stories that have important messages or things that we can learn. Mention that the characters in fables are usually animals. Show the cover of *Fables* and read the title and the

Being a Writer™ **Teacher**

You can either have the students work with their *Being a Writer* partner or assign them a different partner for the *Making Meaning* lessons.

author's name aloud. Show the table of contents and point out that there are several fables in the book.

 ## Introduce "The Camel Dances"

Show the illustration on page 23, read the title "The Camel Dances," and explain that the main character in this fable is a camel that loves ballet dancing. Tell the students that you will read the fable twice. During the first reading they will close their eyes and visualize the story.

 ## Read "The Camel Dances" Aloud with Visualizing

Read "The Camel Dances" aloud, stopping as described below. Do not read the moral of the fable.

Suggested Vocabulary

pirouettes, relevés, arabesques: types of ballet movements (p. 22)

fatigue: great tiredness (p. 22)

recital: performance by musicians or dancers (p. 22)

critic: person who has the job of judging all kinds of performances (p. 22)

ELL Vocabulary

English Language Learners may benefit from discussing additional vocabulary, including:

had her heart set on becoming a ballet dancer: wanted very much to be a ballet dancer (p. 22)

thing of grace: smooth and easy movement (p. 22)

splendid: excellent (p. 22)

◀ **Teacher Note**

The reason for not reading the moral of the story is to allow the students to come up with their own ideas about what is important.

Stop after:

> **p. 22**   "There was no applause."

 Have the students use "Turn to Your Partner" to talk about what they picture happening in the story so far.

Without sharing as a class, reread the last sentence before the stop, and continue reading to the end of the fable. (Remember not to read the moral.)

First in pairs, and then as a class, have the students talk about what they pictured as they listened to the story. Ask questions such as:

Q *What did you picture happening in the story?*

Q *How did you picture the camel?*

5 Reread the Fable

Tell the students that you will reread "The Camel Dances." Explain that this time, as you read, you would like them to think about what the camel learns in the story.

Reread the fable without reading the moral.

6 Discuss Important Ideas in the Fable

Remind the students that fables usually have an important idea or message. Ask:

Q *What important idea or message do you think people can learn from the camel? What in the story makes you think that?*

 Have the students use "Think, Pair, Share" to discuss the question. Then have two or three students share their thinking with the class.

> **Students might say:**
>
> "I think the camel is showing that you should do what makes you happy. The reason I think this is that the camel keeps dancing."
>
> "In addition to what [Sethary] said, I think that the camel doesn't care what her friends think because she likes to dance."

 ELL Note

Understanding the morals of the fables read aloud this week might be challenging for your English Language Learners. Consider explaining each fable to your students prior to these discussions.

7 Discuss the Moral of the Fable

Explain that Arnold Lobel wrote a moral, or message, for the fable. Read the moral aloud and record it on the board.

"Satisfaction will come to those who please themselves."

Facilitate a discussion about the statement, using questions such as:

Q *What does it mean to be satisfied? What do you think "Satisfaction will come to those who please themselves" means?*

Point out that readers often get different important ideas from a fable or have the same idea but express it differently.

Tell the students that they will hear another fable in the next lesson.

INDIVIDUALIZED DAILY READING

8 ▶ **Review the "Reading Comprehension Strategies" Chart and Read Independently**

Direct the students' attention to the "Reading Comprehension Strategies" chart and remind them that these are the strategies they have learned so far this year. Ask them to notice which strategies they use and where they use them during their reading today. Explain that they will use self-stick notes to mark places in their book where they used a particular strategy. At the end of independent reading, they will share in pairs one of the passages and strategies they used. Ask them to be prepared to talk about how the strategy helped them understand what they read.

Distribute a few self-stick notes to each student and have the students read independently for up to 30 minutes, marking places in the reading where they used a comprehension strategy.

As the students read, circulate among them. Ask individual students questions such as:

Q *What is your book about?*

Q *What strategies are you using as you read?*

Q *How does this passage help you [visualize]? How does [visualizing] this passage help you understand the story?*

FACILITATION TIP

During this unit, we invite you to continue practicing **responding neutrally** with interest during class discussions. This week continue to respond neutrally by refraining from overtly praising or criticizing the students' responses. Try responding neutrally by nodding, asking them to say more about their thinking, or asking other students to respond.

Reading Comprehension Strategies

- making connections

At the end of independent reading, have each student share a passage she marked and the strategy she used with her partner. Remind the students to explain their thinking and to ask each other clarifying questions.

As partners share, circulate and listen to their conversations and make notes. You might want to share some of your observations or have a few volunteers share with the class.

Day 2

Read-aloud/Strategy Lesson

In this lesson, the students:

- *Visualize* a story
- Explore important ideas in the story
- Connect important ideas to their own lives
- Read independently for up to 30 minutes
- Give reasons for their ideas

1 ▶ Introduce the Prompt for Supporting Ideas

Have partners sit together. Remind them that in the previous lesson they talked about important ideas in a fable.

Write the prompt "The reason I think this is _____" on the board. Tell the students that you want them to use this prompt when they answer a question or give an opinion about the reading.

Point out that the students have already been practicing this skill when they have answered questions like "Why do you think so?" and "What in the story makes you think that?" Now you would like them to use the prompt themselves rather than wait to be asked why. Encourage them to use the prompt in both partner and whole-class discussions.

2 ▶ Introduce "The Mouse at the Seashore"

Show the cover of *Fables* and explain that you will read another fable written and illustrated by Arnold Lobel. Open the book to pages 40–41, read the title aloud, and show the illustration. Tell the students that this story is titled "The Mouse at the Seashore" and that it is another fable about following a dream.

Explain that you will read the fable aloud twice and that during the first reading, you would like the students to close their eyes and visualize the story.

Materials

- "The Mouse at the Seashore" in *Fables* (pages 40–41)
- "Reading Comprehension Strategies" chart
- Small self-stick notes for each student

3 ▶ Read "The Mouse at the Seashore" Aloud and Visualize

Ask the students to close their eyes. Read "The Mouse at the Seashore" aloud, stopping as described below.

> **Suggested Vocabulary**
>
> **contentment:** feeling of being satisfied or happy (p. 40)
>
> **ELL Vocabulary**
>
> English Language Learners may benefit from discussing additional vocabulary, including:
>
> **alarmed:** frightened (p. 40)
>
> **terrors:** very frightening things (p. 40)
>
> **came to know trouble and fear:** had a difficult, scary time (p. 40)

Stop after:

p. 40 "He was tired and frightened."

 Have the students use "Turn to Your Partner" to talk about what has happened in the story so far. Without sharing as a class, ask:

Q *What do you think will happen to the mouse?*

Have two or three students share their thinking with the class.

Reread the last sentence before the stop and continue reading to the end of the fable. Do not read the moral.

 First in pairs, and then as a class, have the students talk about what they pictured as they listened to the story. Ask questions such as:

Q *What did you picture happening in the story?*

Q *How did you picture the mouse at the end?*

Reread the Fable

Tell the students that you will reread the fable. Explain that this time you would like them to think about the important message in it.

Reread the fable without reading the moral.

Discuss Important Ideas in the Fable

Remind the students that fables have something important to tell the reader. Ask:

Q *What is an important idea in this fable? Explain your thinking.*

Have the students use "Think, Pair, Share" to discuss the question. Then have a few students share their thinking with the class. Remind them to use the prompt "The reason I think this is _____" to explain their thinking, both in pairs and with the whole class.

Discuss and Make Connections with the Moral of the Fable

Read the moral of the fable aloud and record it on the board.

> "All the miles of a hard road are worth a moment of true happiness."

Explain that this is the message that Arnold Lobel wrote for the fable. Facilitate a discussion about the moral by asking questions such as:

Q *What does the story tell us about doing difficult things?*

Q *Have you ever worked really hard to accomplish or finish something and felt very happy when you were done? Explain what happened.*

Reflect on Using the Prompt

Facilitate a brief discussion about how the students did using the prompt to give reasons for their ideas. Share your own observations and explain that you would like the students to continue to focus on giving reasons for their ideas throughout the week.

INDIVIDUALIZED DAILY READING

Discuss Reading Comprehension Strategies

Continue to have the students use self-stick notes to mark places in their books where they use reading comprehension strategies. Have the "Reading Comprehension Strategies" chart posted for the students' reference.

Have the students read independently for up to 30 minutes.

As the students read, circulate among them. Ask individual students question such as:

Q *What is your book about?*

Q *What strategies are you using as you read?*

Q *How does this passage help you [infer]?*

Q *How does [inferring] help you understand the story?*

 At the end of independent reading, have partners each share a passage they marked and the strategy they used. Remind the students to explain their thinking and to ask each other clarifying questions.

Allow time for any student who has finished a book to record it in the "Reading Log" section of his *Student Response Book*.

EXTENSION

Make Connections Between Texts

Show the students the cover of *Wilma Unlimited* (from Unit 5) and remind them that when they read this book they talked about what they could learn from Wilma Rudolph's life. Quickly review by asking:

Q *What were some things we thought we could learn from Wilma Rudolph about how we want to be in our own lives?*

Have a few students share their thinking with the class. Discuss:

Q *How does the story of the mouse and the seashore remind you of the story of Wilma Rudolph?*

Day 3

Materials

- "The Young Rooster" in *Fables* (pages 36–37)
- *Student Response Book* pages 57–61
- *Assessment Resource Book*
- "Reading Comprehension Strategies" chart and a marker
- Small self-stick notes for each student

Guided Strategy Practice

In this lesson, the students:

- *Visualize* a story
- *Explore important ideas* in the story
- Connect important ideas to their own lives
- Read independently for up to 30 minutes
- Give reasons for their ideas
- Learn "Think, Pair, Write"

1 ▶ Review the Prompt for Supporting Thinking

Have partners sit together. Explain that today the students will again talk in pairs and as a whole class. Remind them to focus on giving reasons for their ideas using the prompt "The reason I think this is _____." Explain that at the end of the lesson you will ask them to report how they did giving reasons for their thinking.

2 ▶ Introduce "The Young Rooster"

Explain that they will hear another fable by Arnold Lobel. Tell them that you will read the fable twice. During the first reading, they will visualize the story. During the second reading, they will follow along in their *Student Response Books* and think about the important messages in the fable.

Show the illustration on page 36 and read the title "The Young Rooster."

3 ▶ Read "The Young Rooster" Aloud

Read "The Young Rooster" aloud, stopping as described.

Stop after:

p. 37   "'We need our sunshine!' shouted a Sheep."

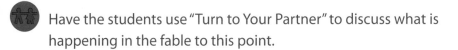 Have the students use "Turn to Your Partner" to discuss what is happening in the fable to this point.

Reread the last sentence and continue reading to the end of the fable, but do not read the moral.

First in pairs, and then as a class, have the students discuss:

Q *What did you picture happening in the fable?*

4 ▶ Reread the Fable

Have the students open to *Student Response Book* pages 57–60, "The Young Rooster." Explain that this is the fable that you read aloud. Ask the students to follow along as you reread the fable aloud and think about what the important message in it is.

Reread "The Young Rooster" aloud. Do not read the moral.

5 ▶ Use "Think, Pair, Write" to Explore Important Ideas

Briefly explain that the students will learn a new cooperative strategy, called "Think, Pair, Write," to think and write about the important messages in "The Young Rooster." Tell the students that "Think, Pair, Write" is very similar to "Think, Pair, Share." In "Think, Pair, Write" they think quietly for a few moments, talk with a partner about their thinking, and then individually write what they are thinking.

Ask the students to think quietly about the important ideas in the fable.

After a few moments, have the students open their *Student Response Books* to page 61, "Think, Pair, Write About 'The Young Rooster.'" Remind the students to give reasons for their thinking. Have partners discuss their thinking; then have each student write her ideas on *Student Response Book* page 61.

CLASS COMPREHENSION ASSESSMENT

Circulate as partners write. Ask yourself:

Q *Are the students able to identify what they think is important in the text?*

Q *Are they able to give reasons for their ideas?*

Record your observations on page 26 of the *Assessment Resource Book*.

After a few minutes, have partners share their writing.

6 ▶ Discuss Important Ideas as a Class

Facilitate a whole-class discussion using the following questions. Remind the students to use "The reason I think this is _____" during this discussion.

Q *What is an important idea or message in this story?*

> **Students might say:**
>
> "I wrote that the story is about not giving up even when it isn't going well. The reason I think this is that the rooster keeps trying to crow."
>
> "In addition to what [Judi] wrote, I think that another important message is that even if other people are unhappy with your job you should not give up. The reason I think this is that once he crowed, his friends weren't very happy because he was too loud."
>
> "I think that the message is almost the same as the one in 'The Camel Dances.' The camel's friends laughed at her and the rooster's friends are upset with him, but both the camel and the rooster are proud of themselves."

Encourage the students to build on each other's thinking by asking questions such as:

Q *Do you agree or disagree with [Peter]? Why?*

Q *What question do you want to ask [Peter] to better understand [his] thinking?*

Teacher Note ▶

The students may have different ideas about what is important in the fable. Encourage them to explain their thinking and refer to the fable's text to support their ideas.

Review Thinking About Important Ideas

Point out that this week the students have been thinking about the important ideas in fables to help them remember and better understand the stories. They have also been using other strategies they know, like visualizing the stories and using clues in the text to infer the important ideas.

Refer to the "Reading Comprehension Strategies" chart and quickly review the strategies the students have learned and used. Add *exploring important ideas* to the chart. Explain that the students will continue to think about important ideas in the coming lessons.

 Reflect on Giving Reasons for Ideas

Facilitate a brief discussion of how the students did giving reasons for their ideas.

Explain that *Fables* will be available for them to read during Individualized Daily Reading.

INDIVIDUALIZED DAILY READING

 Discuss Reading Comprehension Strategies/ Document IDR Conferences

Have the students read independently for up to 30 minutes.

Continue to have the students use self-stick notes to mark places they use reading comprehension strategies. Use the "IDR Conference Notes" record sheet to conduct and document individual conferences.

 At the end of independent reading, have partners share a passage they marked and the strategies they used to help them understand it. Remind the students to use the prompt to explain their thinking and to ask each other clarifying questions.

> *Reading Comprehension Strategies*
>
> - making connections

EXTENSIONS

Read Other Fables

Read more fables from *Fables* or from other books. Some authors who have written fables or legends are Aesop, Leo Lionni, and Tomie de Paola.

Read About Arnold Lobel

The book *Meet the Authors and Illustrators (Volume One),* by Deborah Kovacs and James Preller, includes a brief biography of Arnold Lobel. Read the selection aloud and have the students discuss some of the important ideas in the article. You may also want to read other books by this author.

Day 4

Class Meeting

In this lesson, the students:

- Review the ground rules and procedure for a class meeting
- Discuss how class meetings help create a safe and caring community
- Read independently for up to 30 minutes
- Give reasons for their thinking
- Practice "Think, Pair, Write"

1 Gather for a Class Meeting

Have the students gather for a class meeting with partners sitting together, and ask them to make sure that they can see all their classmates. Review the ground rules and explain that at the end of the meeting the students will talk about how they did following the rules.

Remind the students to use the prompts they have learned to help them add to and clarify one another's thinking and to give reasons for their own thinking. Ask and briefly discuss:

Q *What can we do to make sure everyone who wants to share gets a chance to do so?*

2 Discuss How the Students Are Creating a Caring Community

Explain that the purpose of this class meeting is to check in on how the students are doing creating a caring community.

Materials

- Space for the class to sit in a circle
- "Class Meeting Ground Rules" chart
- *Student Response Book* page 62
- Small self-stick notes for each student
- *Student Response Book*, IDR Journal section

> Class Meeting
> Ground Rules
>
> - one person talks
>   at a time
> - listen to one another

Have the students use "Think, Pair, Share" to think about and discuss:

Q *What have you done to help create a safe and caring reading community?*

As the students share, probe their thinking with follow-up questions such as:

Q *What is working well during our partner and whole-class discussions?*

Q *What do you think we need to work on?*

> **Students might say:**
>
> "When my partner asked me a question, it showed me she was listening and thinking about what I said."
>
> "When my partner gives reasons for his ideas, it helps me understand his thinking."
>
> "I think we could use the prompt 'The reason I think that is _____' more to help explain our thinking during class discussions."
>
> "I agree with [Grady]. I think we should use the discussion prompts more also."

Q *How are we being responsible during IDR?*

If a topic comes up during today's class meeting that requires more time for discussion than is available, make note of it and tell the students that they will continue the discussion during another class meeting. Schedule a follow-up class meeting in the next few days to continue the discussion. Adjourn the class meeting and have the students return to their desks, with partners sitting together.

 3 ▶ **Use "Think, Pair, Write" to Reflect on Class Meetings**

Review "Think, Pair, Write" and explain that the students will use this technique to write about why class meetings are important. Ask the students to think quietly about the questions on the following page.

Q *Why are class meetings important?*

Q *How do they help us build a caring and safe reading community?*

After a few moments, have the students open their *Student Response Books* to page 62, "Think, Pair, Write About Why Class Meetings Are Important." Ask the students to discuss their thinking in pairs, and then individually write their ideas on the *Student Response Book* page. Remind the students to give reasons for their thinking.

After a few minutes, have partners share what they have written.

4 ▶ Discuss the Writing as a Class

Use the following questions to facilitate a whole-class discussion.

Q *If you were to tell someone about why class meetings are important, what would you tell them?*

Q *What do you like about class meetings? How do they help create a safe and caring community?*

Students might say:

"I think that class meetings are important because we get to talk about how things are going in our class."

"I agree with [Yolanda], and I think that the class meetings have helped us get to know one another better."

"In addition to what [Yolanda and Kevin] said, I would tell someone that class meetings help us solve problems together."

Explain that the class will continue to work on building a safe and caring reading community.

INDIVIDUALIZED DAILY READING

 Write About Reading Comprehension Strategies in Their IDR Journals

Explain to the students that today they will continue to use self-stick notes to mark passages where they use comprehension strategies to help them understand what they are reading.

Have the students read independently for up to 30 minutes.

At the end of independent reading, have the students write about their reading and a strategy they used—the name of the strategy, where they used it, and how it helped them understand—in their IDR Journals. Have a few students share their writing with the class.

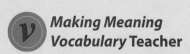

Making Meaning Vocabulary **Teacher**

Next week you will revisit *Fables* to teach Vocabulary Week 23.

Week 2

Overview

UNIT 8: DETERMINING IMPORTANT IDEAS

Fiction and Expository Nonfiction

Lifetimes

by David L. Rice, illustrated by Michael S. Maydak
(Dawn Publications, 1997)

This book is a collection of short descriptions of the lifetimes of different species, and the lessons each has to teach.

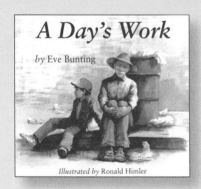

A Day's Work*

by Eve Bunting, illustrated by Ronald Himler
(Clarion, 1994)

A young Mexican American boy named Francisco helps his grandfather find work and learns a valuable lesson about integrity.

*This book was also used in Unit 4.

ALTERNATIVE BOOKS

The Lion and the Mouse: An Aesop Fable
retold by Bernadette Watts

Luba and the Wren by Patricia Polacco

Comprehension Focus

- Students *explore important ideas* in a text.

- Students *make inferences* to understand a text.

- Students *synthesize* by interpreting a text's message or theme.

- Students read independently.

Social Development Focus

- Students relate the value of respect to their behavior.

- Students develop the group skill of giving reasons for their ideas.

DO AHEAD

- Prepare to model identifying important ideas in independent reading (see Day 3, Step 2 on page 438).

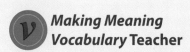

Making Meaning Vocabulary Teacher

If you are teaching Developmental Studies Center's *Making Meaning Vocabulary* program, teach Vocabulary Week 23 this week. For more information, see the *Making Meaning Vocabulary Teacher's Manual.*

Day 1

Materials

- "A lifetime for an army ant is about three years" in *Lifetimes* (page 6)

Read-aloud/Strategy Lesson

In this lesson, the students:

- *Explore important ideas* in nonfiction texts
- Connect important ideas to their own lives
- Read independently for up to 30 minutes
- Give reasons for their ideas

▶ 1 Review Important Ideas and Making Inferences

Have partners sit together. Review that last week they heard and discussed some fables and talked about the important ideas in each one. Explain that most stories and poems have important ideas or messages for the reader to think about. Tell the students that for the next few weeks they will continue to think about the important ideas in stories or books. Point out that readers often use inference to determine what is important. Ask:

Q *What do we mean when we talk about inferring or making an inference?*

Have a few students share their thinking with the class.

> **Students might say:**
>
> "It's when the author doesn't say it but you figure it out from the story."
>
> "Inferring means using clues in the text to understand the characters better."
>
> "When you infer, you use clues to figure out what the author wants you to know about something."

Teacher Note ▶

If the students have trouble answering the question, prompt them with ideas like those in the "Students might say" note or give an example from a previous read-aloud.

▶ 2 Introduce *Lifetimes*

Show the cover of *Lifetimes* and read the names of the author and illustrator aloud. Explain that a lifetime is how long an animal or plant can be expected to live. (For example, a lifetime for a human being is about 85 years.) Explain that it is a book about what we can learn from the lives of animals.

▶3 Introduce the Topic of Ants and Share Background Knowledge

Show the illustration on page 6 of *Lifetimes* and explain that today you will read aloud a section of the book about army ants. Ask:

Q *What do you think you already know about ants?*

Have two or three students share their thinking with the class.

> **Students might say:**
>
> "They always walk in a line."
>
> "They're very small and they like food."
>
> "If you step on an anthill all the ants swarm out."

▶4 Read Aloud and Discuss What the Students Learned

Explain that you will read the passage about ants twice. During the first reading, they will think about what they learn about army ants, and then talk in pairs about what they learned.

Read page 6, "A lifetime for an army ant is about three years," without reading the last sentence.

> **Suggested Vocabulary**
>
> **cockroaches:** brown or black insects that live in warm, dark places (p. 6)
> **pests:** creatures that bother or destroy other animals or plants (p. 6)
>
> **ELL Vocabulary**
>
> English Language Learners may benefit from discussing additional vocabulary, including:
>
> **"ant bridge":** (refer to the illustration on p. 6)
> **"ant ball":** a group of ants clinging together so that they can float across the water (p. 6)

Stop after:

> **p. 6**   "When they return their houses are completely free of rats, cockroaches, or other pests."

Without reading the last sentence ("Army ants show us…"), ask:

Q *What are some interesting things you learned about army ants?*

 Have the students use "Turn to Your Partner" to discuss what they learned. Have two or three students share their thinking with the class.

Teacher Note

To maintain the flow of the lesson, have only two or three students share after the first reading. Hearing others recall facts from the passage will help the students remember what they learned.

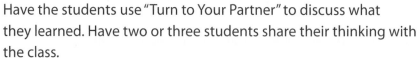 **5** ▶ **Reread and Discuss the Important Message**

Explain that you will read the passage again. Remind the students that last week they read fables and thought about the important ideas or messages in them. Explain that as you reread the passage, you would like them to think about what important lesson people can learn from army ants.

Teacher Note ▶

Omitting the author's "message" allows the students to generate their own ideas about what is important in the text.

Reread the passage aloud without reading the last line. After the reading, ask:

Q *What important lesson can we learn from army ants? What in the text makes you think that?*

 Have the students use "Think, Pair, Share" to discuss their ideas. Remind them to use the prompt "The reason I think this is _____" when talking in pairs. Have two or three students share their thinking with the class.

> ***Students might say:***
>
> "You should help other people when they need help. The reason I think this is that the army ants make a bridge to get across the river."
>
> "When people work as a team, they can do more. The reason I think this is that the ants make an ant ball."

Connect the Reading to Classroom Community

Facilitate a brief discussion using the following questions:

Q *What are some things we do in our classroom community that remind you of the way the ants live?*

Q *What are some things we can do in our classroom community to be more like the ants?*

Let the students know that in the next lesson they will hear a passage about a different kind of animal.

INDIVIDUALIZED DAILY READING

7 Think About and Discuss Important Messages

Remind the students that they have been using inference to think about important messages in fables and nonfiction texts. Explain that today you want them to think about some of the important messages or ideas in the stories they are reading independently.

Have the students read independently for up to 30 minutes. As the students read, circulate among them. Ask individual students questions such as:

Q *What is your book about?*

Q *What do you think the author wants the reader to realize or think about?*

Q *What can you learn about life from this book?*

At the end of independent reading, have a few volunteers share the important messages or ideas in their story or book.

EXTENSION

Do the Activities on Page 6 of *Lifetimes*

Have the students explore the follow-up activities on page 6 of *Lifetimes*: "Tell about it," "Think about it," and "Look it up."

Day 2

Guided Strategy Practice

In this lesson, the students:

- *Explore important ideas* in a nonfiction text
- Connect important ideas to their own lives
- Read independently for up to 30 minutes
- Give reasons for their ideas

Materials

- "A lifetime for an elephant is about 65 years" in *Lifetimes* (page 19)
- *Student Response Book* page 63
- *Assessment Resource Book*
- (Optional) *Student Response Book* page 64
- *Student Response Book*, IDR Journal section

1 ▶ Review Giving Reasons for Ideas

Remind the students that in the last two weeks they have been using the prompt "The reason I think this is _____" to explain their thinking. Ask:

Q *How does it help you when your partner explains [her] thinking to you?*

Have two or three students share their thinking with the class, and encourage the students to continue to practice giving reasons for their opinions today.

> **Students might say:**
>
> "I can understand my partner better."
>
> "If my partner explains, I might get a different idea."

2 ▶ Introduce Elephants and Share Background Knowledge

Show the illustration on page 19 and explain that today you will read aloud a section of *Lifetimes* about elephants. Ask:

Q *What do you think you already know about elephants?*

Have two or three students share their thinking with the class.

Students might say:

"They squirt water with their trunks."

"They're very big."

"I've seen them do tricks at the circus."

3 ▶ Read Aloud and Discuss What the Students Learned

Explain that you will read the passage about elephants twice. During the first reading, the students will think about what they are learning about elephants, and then they will talk in pairs about what they learned.

Read page 19, "A lifetime for an elephant is about 65 years," without reading the last sentence.

> **Suggested Vocabulary**
>
> **trumpeting sounds:** loud noises that sound like a horn (p. 19)
> **injured:** hurt or harmed (p. 19)
> **moaning:** making a sad, crying sound (p. 19)

Stop after:

p. 19 "Without water these animals would die."

Without reading the last sentence ("Elephants remind us…"), ask:

Q *What are some interesting things you learned about elephants?*

 Have the students use "Turn to Your Partner" to discuss what they learned.

4 ▶ Reread and Write About the Important Message

Explain that you will read the passage again. Remind the students that yesterday they thought about what lessons they could learn from army ants.

Have the students open their *Student Response Books* to page 63. Explain that as you reread the passage you would like them to follow along and think about important lessons people can learn from elephants. After the reading, they will talk in pairs, and then write about their ideas.

Reread the passage aloud without reading the last sentence. After the reading, ask:

Q *What lesson might the author want people to learn from elephants? What in the text makes you think that?*

 Have the students use "Think, Pair, Write" to discuss and record their ideas at the bottom of the page. Remind them to use the prompt "The reason I think this is _____" in talking with their partners and in their writing.

◀ **Teacher Note**

If necessary, review the procedure for "Think, Pair, Write."

> ### CLASS COMPREHENSION ASSESSMENT
>
> Circulate among the students and ask yourself:
>
> **Q** *Can the students use the text to infer important ideas?*
>
> **Q** *Can the students support their thinking with evidence from the text?*
>
> Record your observations on page 27 of the *Assessment Resource Book.*

▶5 Share and Discuss Writing About Important Ideas

 When the students have finished writing, have partners read their writing to one another and discuss briefly what they wrote.

Have two or three students share with the class their ideas about what people can learn from elephants.

> **Students might say:**
>
> "I think the author is telling us that we should care about others. The reason I think this is that the elephants take care of other elephants who are sick, and they get very sad if another elephant dies."

6 Discuss What the Students Wonder About Elephants

Remind the students that they have been spending a lot of time thinking about what they learn from reading books and stories. Explain that learning more about something can also make readers wonder about it. Explain that good readers often have questions, even when they're finished reading something. Ask them to think for a minute about what they still want to know about elephants. Ask:

Q *What do you still wonder about elephants?*

Have a few students share their thinking with the class. Encourage interested students to do their own research about elephants or do the "Read About Elephants" extension activity. Let the students know that if they want to read about other animals, *Lifetimes* will be available in the classroom library.

Teacher Note

If the students need additional practice with identifying important ideas, repeat this lesson using page 20 in *Lifetimes* and *Student Response Book* page 64.

INDIVIDUALIZED DAILY READING

7 Write About Important Messages in Their IDR Journals

Explain that today you want the students to think about the important messages or ideas in the stories they are reading. At the end of independent reading, they will each write about an important message in their book.

Have the students read independently for up to 30 minutes. As the students read, circulate among them. Ask individual students questions such as:

Q *What is your book about?*

Q *What do you think the author wants the reader to realize or think about?*

Q *What can you learn about life from this book?*

At the end of independent reading, have each student write in his IDR Journal about an important message in his book.

EXTENSIONS

Read About Elephants

Gather a variety of reading materials about elephants for independent reading. Give the students time to read and share some important ideas about elephants with the class.

Do the Activities on Page 19 of *Lifetimes*

Have the students explore the follow-up activities on page 19 of *Lifetimes,* "Tell about it," "Think about it," and "Look it up."

Day 3

Materials

- *A Day's Work* (from Unit 4, Week 2)
- Narrative texts at appropriate levels for independent reading
- Small self-stick notes for each student

Teacher Note

In this lesson, you will use pages 28–32 in *A Day's Work* to model identifying important ideas or messages.

Independent Strategy Practice

In this lesson, the students:

- *Explore important ideas* in texts read independently
- Give reasons for their ideas

1 ▶ Review the Week

Review that readers can make sense of what they read by thinking about important ideas or messages in books. Often, authors don't directly state important ideas or messages, and readers must infer them from the text. Explain that today the students will practice thinking about important ideas in the books they read independently.

2 ▶ Model Identifying Important Ideas and Messages with *A Day's Work*

Show the cover of *A Day's Work* and read the title and the author's name. Remind the students that they heard this story about a boy and his grandfather earlier in the year. Ask the students to watch as you use the book to model thinking about important ideas.

Read pages 28–32 aloud. Think aloud about what the author's message might be. (You might say, "Francisco feels sad because he lied to get work for his grandfather, but then he feels better. I'm going to put a sticky note where it says 'Francisco had begun to understand the important things too.' I think the author's message is that people should be honest and take responsibility for their own mistakes.")

3 ▶ Read Independently Without Stopping

Distribute two self-stick notes to each student. Have the students open their books and mark the place they begin reading today with a self-stick note. Have them read independently for 10 minutes.

4 ▶ Retell in Pairs

Stop the students after 10 minutes. Ask partners to tell each other the titles of the books they are reading, the authors' names, and what the books are about. Then have partners briefly tell each other what happened in the part of the story they just read.

5 ▶ Reread Independently and Talk to a Partner

Explain that the students will reread the part of the story they just read and mark with a self-stick note a place in the book where they think something important is happening or where there is something the author wants them to think about.

Have the students reread and stop them after 10 minutes. Have them use "Turn to Your Partner" to discuss the part they marked and why they think that part is important. Remind them to use the prompt "The reason I think this is _____" in their conversations.

6 ▶ Discuss Important Ideas as a Class

Have several volunteers share the important ideas or messages they identified. Remind each student to say the title and author of her book. Probe the students' thinking by asking:

Q *What is your book about? What happened in the part you read today?*

Q *What part did you mark as important? Why do you think it is important?*

Share any observations you made of how partners did working together and explain that the students will continue to talk with their partners about important ideas and messages in their independent reading books.

◀ **Teacher Note**

Circulate as the students reread and look for evidence that they are able to identify what is important. If a students is having difficulty, you might ask her questions such as:

Q *What is happening in the part of the book you just read?*

Q *What do you think is important to know or remember about what happened?*

Q *What do you think the author is telling you?*

Day 4

Materials

- Narrative texts at appropriate levels for independent reading
- Small self-stick notes for each student

Independent Strategy Practice

In this lesson, the students:

- *Explore important ideas* in texts read independently
- Give reasons for their ideas
- Act respectfully toward one another

1 ▶ Get Ready to Read Independently

Explain that today the students will spend more time thinking about the important ideas in the books they are reading independently. Ask:

Q *What are some things we can do to be respectful of one another during independent reading?*

Have two or three students share their thinking with the class. Tell them that you will check in with them at the end of the lesson to see how they did.

2 ▶ Read Independently Without Stopping

Have the students open their books and mark the place they begin reading with a self-stick note. Have them read independently for 10 minutes.

3 ▶ Retell in Pairs

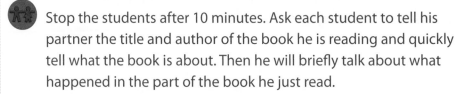

Stop the students after 10 minutes. Ask each student to tell his partner the title and author of the book he is reading and quickly tell what the book is about. Then he will briefly talk about what happened in the part of the book he just read.

4 Reread Independently and Talk to a Partner

Explain that the students will reread, starting again at the self-stick note, and mark with another self-stick note a place in the story where they think something important is happening or where there is something important the author wants them to think about.

Have the students reread and stop them after 10 minutes. Have them use "Turn to Your Partner" to discuss what they marked and why they think that part is important. Remind them to use the prompt "The reason I think this is _____" in their conversations.

◀ **Teacher Note**

If the students need additional support identifying important ideas, model the procedure again with a narrative text of your choice.

5 Discuss Important Ideas as a Class

Have several volunteers share the important ideas or messages they identified. Remind them each to say the title and author of their book. Probe the students' thinking by asking:

Q *What is your book about? What happened in the part you read today?*

Q *What part did you mark as important? Why do you think it is important?*

6 Talk About Working Together

Ask:

Q *How did you do today being respectful of one another during independent reading?*

Have two or three students share their thinking with the class. Share any observations you made of students acting responsibly. Explain that they will continue to think about important ideas and messages in the next week.

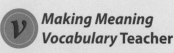

***Making Meaning Vocabulary* Teacher**

Next week you will revisit *Lifetimes* to teach Vocabulary Week 24.

Week 3

Overview

UNIT 8: DETERMINING IMPORTANT IDEAS
Fiction and Expository Nonfiction

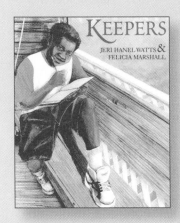

Keepers

by Jeri Hanel Watts, illustrated by Felicia Marshall
(Lee & Low, 1997)

After Kenyon regrets spending the money that he saved for his grandmother's birthday present, he comes up with a more interesting idea for a gift.

ALTERNATIVE BOOKS

Your Move by Eve Bunting

The Wednesday Surprise by Eve Bunting

Comprehension Focus

• Students *explore important ideas* in texts.

• Students *make inferences* to understand texts.

• Students *synthesize* by interpreting a text's message or theme.

• Students read independently.

Social Development Focus

• Students take responsibility for their learning and behavior.

• Students develop the group skills of giving reasons for their ideas and asking clarifying questions.

DO AHEAD

• Collect narrative texts at a variety of reading levels for the students to read independently.

• Make copies of the Unit 8 Parent Letter (BLM22) to send home with the students on the last day of the unit.

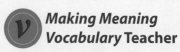

Making Meaning Vocabulary Teacher

If you are teaching Developmental Studies Center's *Making Meaning Vocabulary* program, teach Vocabulary Week 24 this week. For more information, see the *Making Meaning Vocabulary Teacher's Manual*.

Materials

• *Keepers* (pages 1–20)

Read-aloud

In this lesson, the students:

• Hear and discuss a story
• *Explore important ideas* in the story
• Read independently for up to 30 minutes
• Give reasons for their ideas

▶1 Review Important Ideas

Have partners sit together. Remind the students that in the previous lessons they listened to short passages about different animals and talked about the important things people can learn from animals' lives.

Explain that this week they will continue to think about important messages or ideas in fiction stories.

▶2 Introduce *Keepers*

Show the cover of *Keepers* and read the title and the author's and illustrator's names aloud. Explain that this is a story about a boy, Kenyon, and his grandmother, Little Dolly. Tell the students that they will learn the meaning of the title, *Keepers,* during the read-aloud. Ask:

Q *What do you think* keepers *might mean?*

▶3 Read the First Part of *Keepers* Aloud

Read pages 1–20 of *Keepers* aloud, showing the illustrations and stopping as described on the next page.

Suggested Vocabulary

familiar: well-known (p. 4)

stroke: sudden lack of oxygen to the brain caused by the blocking or breaking of a blood vessel (p. 4)

reminder: something that helps a person remember (p. 6)

wallop-bat day: (made-up word) a great day—a good day for hitting baseballs (p. 9)

clenched: squeezed (p. 11)

tribe: group of people who share the same ancestors, customs, and laws (p. 13)

antique store: store selling old objects, such as furniture, dishes, and jewelry (p. 19)

rich aroma: very good smell (p. 20)

ELL Vocabulary

English Language Learners may benefit from discussing additional vocabulary, including:

snoring: breathing noisily while sleeping (p. 4)

tip-toed: walked quietly on his toes (p. 6)

muttering: speaking in a low, unclear way with the mouth nearly closed (p. 9)

clean out of the park: hit the baseball out of the park, most likely over the fence (p. 9)

park diamond: baseball field (p. 11)

weaves the tale: tells the story (p. 13)

legends: stories about the past that might be true (p. 13)

headed out: went out (p. 15)

tourists: people who travel for pleasure (p. 19)

storefronts: side of stores facing the street (p. 20)

◀ **Teacher Note**

If necessary, be prepared to help the students with the dialect in the story.

Stop after:

p. 9   "She was a big-boned woman with great big hands and a great big voice and a great lot of words."

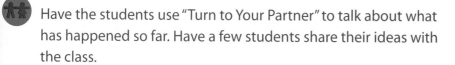

Have the students use "Turn to Your Partner" to talk about what has happened so far. Have a few students share their ideas with the class.

Reread the last sentence before the stop and continue reading to the next stop:

p. 13   "'Lord, honey, that's nice, but you a boy. I got to find me a girl Keeper. You cain't be a Keeper if you a boy.'"

Have the students use "Turn to Your Partner" to discuss what has happened in the story and what they learned about the meaning of the title, *Keepers*. Have a few students share their ideas with the class.

Reread the last sentence before the previous stop and continue reading to the end of page 20.

4 ▶ Discuss the Story as a Class

Facilitate a whole-class discussion of the story, using the questions that follow. Remind the students to use "The reason I think this is _____" and the discussion prompts they have learned to add to one another's thinking.

Q *What seems important in the story so far?*

Q *What do you think might happen in the story?*

> **Students might say:**
>
> "I think it's important that his grandmother thinks only girls can be keepers. The reason I think this is because Kenyon is a boy and he likes his grandmother's stories."
>
> "It is probably important that he spends his money on a baseball glove because now he has a problem—he can't buy his grandmother a gift."
>
> "I think he might change his mind and take the glove back so he can get his grandmother a birthday present. The reason I think this is that he spent all the money he saved for her present."

Ask the students to keep their predictions in mind, and tell them that they will hear the rest of the story tomorrow.

INDIVIDUALIZED DAILY READING

5 ▶ Discuss Important Messages/Document IDR Conferences

 Explain that today you want the students to think about the important messages or ideas in the stories they are reading. At the end of independent reading, they will share in pairs the important messages they inferred from their reading.

Have the students read independently for up to 30 minutes.

As the students read, use the "IDR Conference Notes" record sheet to conduct and document individual conferences.

 At the end of independent reading, have partners share important messages or ideas they inferred from their reading.

Day 2

Materials

- *Keepers* (pages 20–32)
- *Student Response Book,* IDR Journal section

Teacher Note

If the students have trouble recalling clarifying questions, give examples such as:

- *Can you tell me more about that?*
- *What did you mean when you said…?*
- *Can you give me an example of what you mean?*

Teacher Note ▶

If the students have difficulty recalling the story, show the illustrations and ask the students to do a quick retelling as you leaf through the first part of the book.

Read-aloud

In this lesson, the students:

- *Explore important ideas* in a story
- Read independently for up to 30 minutes
- Give reasons for their ideas
- Ask clarifying questions

▶ **1 Discuss Asking Clarifying Questions**

Remind the students that they heard the first part of *Keepers,* and explain that today partners will be talking about something important that happened in the first part of the story. Ask:

Q *If you don't understand your partner, what are some questions you can ask to help you understand what [he] is saying?*

Have two or three students share their thinking with the class.

▶ **2 Talk About Important Ideas in the First Part of *Keepers***

Ask:

Q *What is something that happened in the first part of the story that you think is important? Why do you think that is important?*

Have the students use "Think, Pair, Share" to discuss the question. Then have a few students share their thinking with the class.

Explain that you will read the rest of the story today. Ask the students to listen for important things that happen in the rest of the story.

▶ **3 Read the Second Part of *Keepers* Aloud**

Read pages 20–32 of *Keepers* aloud, showing the illustrations and stopping as described on the next page.

Suggested Vocabulary

assorted chocolates: a variety of chocolate candies (p. 28)

delicately: gently and carefully (p. 30)

bind: fasten together and put a cover on the pages of a book (p. 30)

ELL Vocabulary

English Language Learners may benefit from discussing additional vocabulary, including:

the porch spilled over with people: there were a lot of people on the porch (p. 28)

don't that beat all: (dialect) isn't that amazing (p. 30)

Reread page 20; then continue reading to page 27.

Stop after:

p. 27 "'The stories. That was it. He *could* give her something.'"

Ask:

Q *What do you think Kenyon is going to give her?*

First in pairs, and then as a class, have the students discuss what they are thinking about at this point. Have a few pairs share their ideas with the class.

Reread the last three sentences on page 27 and continue reading to the end of the book.

4 ▶ Discuss the Story as a Class

Remind the students that in past lessons they did a lot of thinking about how characters change in stories. Facilitate a brief discussion about character change in *Keepers* using the questions that follow. Remind the students to give reasons for their thinking and to use the discussion prompts. Ask:

Q *How does Kenyon change in the story?*

Q *How does Little Dolly change in the story?*

Teacher Note   ▶

Encourage the students to engage directly in discussion with one another by asking questions such as:

Q *What questions would you like to ask [Mark] about what he said?*

Q *[Kami] told us she thinks [Little Dolly changes her mind about who can be a keeper]. What can you add to what she said?*

Q *[Jesse] told us he thinks [Kenyon learns to be more responsible]. Do you agree or disagree? Why?*

Have a few volunteers share their ideas. Be prepared to reread parts of the story to support the students' thinking.

Tell the students that they will revisit *Keepers* in the next lesson to think more deeply about important messages in the story.

INDIVIDUALIZED DAILY READING

5 ▶ **Discuss Important Messages/Document IDR Conferences**

Ask the students to think about important messages or ideas in the stories they are reading.

Have the students read independently for up to 30 minutes.

Use the "IDR Conference Notes" record sheet to conduct and document individual conferences.

 At the end of independent reading, have partners share important messages or ideas they inferred from their reading.

EXTENSION

Share a Personal Story

Review that in this book, *keepers* are people who know and keep stories about their families, traditions, or culture and pass them on orally from one generation to the next. Ask the students to think about a story about their family that they would like to share. Explain that the story can be one that they heard from a relative or friend or one from their own experience. Model by sharing a story about your own family. Have the students share their stories.

Day 3

Guided Strategy Practice

In this lesson, the students:

- *Explore important ideas* in a story
- Connect important ideas to their own lives
- Read independently for up to 30 minutes
- Give reasons for their ideas

1▶ Discuss Important Ideas in Longer Texts

Review that this week the students have been thinking about important ideas in *Keepers*. Remind them that they also thought about what important ideas or messages the authors might have intended in fables and nonfiction passages about various animals. Point out that authors sometimes communicate the important ideas or messages at the end of the story. Rereading the end of a story can help readers make sense of what happened earlier in the story. Ask:

Q *What are some important ideas that you remember from* Keepers?

Have a few students share their thinking with the class. Encourage them to keep these ideas in mind as they hear the end of the story again.

2▶ Reread the End of *Keepers*

Reread pages 30–32 of *Keepers* aloud, and then ask the students to open to *Student Response Book* page 65, "Excerpt from *Keepers*." Explain that this is a copy of part of what you read aloud. Ask the students to follow along, and read the excerpt aloud again.

Materials

- *Keepers* (pages 30–32)
- *Student Response Book* pages 65–66
- *Assessment Resource Book*
- *Student Response Book*, IDR Journal section

Discuss Important Ideas in the Excerpt

Facilitate a brief discussion using the following questions:

Q *Why is this ending important?*

Q *Why do you think the author called the book* Keepers?

 "Think, Pair, Write" About Messages in the Story

Tell the students that they will think to themselves for a moment, and then partners will share about the messages in *Keepers*. They will record their ideas in their *Student Response Books*. Have the students turn to *Student Response Book* page 66.

Have the students use "Think, Pair, Write" to discuss and write about the question:

Q *What do you think the author wants people to learn from this story? What happens in the story that makes you think that?*

> **CLASS COMPREHENSION ASSESSMENT**
>
> As the students discuss the question and record their ideas, circulate among them. Ask yourself:
>
> **Q** *Can the students identify important messages in the story?*
>
> **Q** *Can they connect the important ideas to the text?*
>
> **Q** *Can they give reasons for their thinking?*
>
> Record your observations on page 28 of the *Assessment Resource Book*.

 Share and Discuss the Writing

 First in pairs, and then as a class, have the students share their writing. Encourage the students to ask clarifying questions when they don't understand each other's thinking.

Discuss questions such as:

Q *What are the important ideas that you wrote about?*

Q *What do you think the author might say are important ideas in the book? Why?*

Q *Would you like to be the keeper of your family stories? Why or why not?*

Following the class discussion, give the students time to add to or revise their writing in their *Student Response Books.*

6 Reflect on "Think, Pair, Write"

Help the students reflect on their work together by discussing questions such as:

Q *How did "Think, Pair, Write" go for you and your partner today?*

Q *How does it help you to think quietly and talk about your thinking before you start to write your ideas?*

Let the students know that in the next lesson they will have a chance to talk and write about important messages in their own reading.

INDIVIDUALIZED DAILY READING

7 Document IDR Conferences/Have the Students Write About Important Messages in Their IDR Journals

Explain that during IDR today you want the students to think about important messages or ideas in the stories they are reading. At the end of independent reading, they will write about an important message they learned from their books.

Have the students read independently for up to 30 minutes.

Use the "IDR Conference Notes" record sheet to conduct and document individual conferences.

◀ **Teacher Note**

If you feel your students need more guided experience exploring important ideas in narrative text, you might want to repeat this week's Days 1, 2, and 3 lessons with alternative books before going on to Day 4. Alternative books are listed on this week's Overview page. You may also want to have the students repeat Day 4, Independent Strategy Practice.

At the end of independent reading, have each student write in her IDR Journal about an important message in her book.

EXTENSION

Compare Similar Stories

Several of the books you have read earlier in *Making Meaning* depict a relationship between a child and an older relative (*Aunt Flossie's Hats* and *A Day's Work,* for example). Review some of these and have the students discuss the important messages in each book and compare the stories.

Day 4

Independent Strategy Practice

In this lesson, the students:

* *Explore important ideas* in a story read independently
* Give reasons for their ideas

1 Review the Week

Have partners sit together. Review that this week the students heard *Keepers* and thought about what is important in the story. Remind them that readers make sense of what they read by thinking about the important ideas or messages in stories. Explain that today the students will practice thinking and writing about the important ideas and messages in the books they are reading independently.

Also remind the students that they practiced using "The reason I think this is _____" to explain their ideas. Encourage them to continue to practice this today.

2 Read Independently Without Stopping

Ask each student to use a self-stick note to mark the place he begins reading today. Have the students read independently for 10 minutes.

3 Retell in Pairs

Stop the students after 10 minutes. Ask each student to tell her partner the title of the book she is reading and the author's name, and then quickly say what the book is about. Then have partners briefly tell each other what happened in the part of the story they just read.

Materials

* Narrative texts at appropriate levels for independent reading
* Small self-stick notes for each student
* *Student Response Book* page 67
* "Reading Comprehension Strategies" chart
* *Assessment Resource Book*
* Unit 8 Parent Letter (BLM22)

Teacher Note ▶

If necessary, model the procedure again using the procedure you used on page 438 with the book *Keepers*. (For example, you might reread pages 20–23 aloud and say, "I'm going to put a note where it says Kenyon remembers his grandmother and then can't breathe right. I think the author wants me to get the message that Kenyon feels bad about buying the baseball glove.")

Teacher Note

If the students are having difficulty identifying important ideas, ask them questions such as:

Q *What is happening in the part of the book you just read?*

Q *What do you think is important to remember about what happened?*

Q *What might the author be trying to tell you?*

Reading Comprehension Strategies

- making connections

4 ▶ Reread and Discuss Important Ideas

Explain to the students that they will reread and mark with a self-stick note a place in the story where they think something important is happening or where there is something important the author wants them to think about.

Have the students reread. Stop them after 10 minutes and have them use "Turn to Your Partner" to discuss the part they marked and why they think that part is important.

5 ▶ Write About Important Ideas

Ask the students to turn to *Student Response Book* page 67. Explain that they will write about what they marked in their independent reading books. Have them write in their *Student Response Books* about these questions:

Q *What is happening in the part of the story you marked?*

Q *What might the author want you to be thinking about when you read that part?*

6 ▶ Share and Discuss the Writing

First in pairs, and then as a class, have the students share their writing. Encourage the students to ask clarifying questions to help them understand one another's thinking.

Following the class discussion, give the students time to add to or revise their writing in their *Student Response Books*.

7 ▶ Reflect on the Unit

Refer to the "Reading Comprehension Strategies" chart and remind the students that they have been identifying important ideas in books and stories during this unit. Often they used clues in the story to infer what was important or what the story was about. Tell them that thinking about the important ideas helps them remember more and understand what they read at a deeper level.

Tell them that this is the last lesson in which they will work with this partner. Facilitate a brief discussion about how they worked together and give partners an opportunity to thank each other.

INDIVIDUAL COMPREHENSION ASSESSMENT

Before continuing on to Unit 9, take this opportunity to assess individual students' progress in identifying important ideas and messages. Please refer to pages 42–43 in the *Assessment Resource Book* for instructions.

Teacher Note

Note that this is the last week in Unit 8. You will assign new partners for Unit 9.

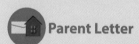 **Parent Letter**

Send home with each student the Parent Letter for this unit (see "Do Ahead," page 443). Periodically, have a few students share with the class what they are reading at home.

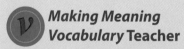 ***Making Meaning Vocabulary* Teacher**

Next week you will revisit *Keepers* to teach Vocabulary Week 25.

Unit 9

Revisiting the Reading Life

During this unit, the students use important ideas to build summaries. They reflect on their growth as readers and as members of a classroom community. They continue to develop the group skills of giving reasons for their opinions and discussing their opinions respectfully. During IDR the students continue to practice self-monitoring and to reflect on the reading strategies they use that help them understand what they are reading. They also have a class meeting to discuss their growth as readers and as members of a classroom community.

Week 1 Student-selected book

Week 1

Overview

UNIT 9: REVISITING THE READING LIFE

Comprehension Focus

• Students *use important ideas* to *build summaries*.

• Students reflect on their growth as readers over the year.

• Students read independently.

Social Development Focus

• Students analyze the effect of their behavior on others and on the group work.

• Students develop the group skills of giving reasons for their opinions and discussing their opinions respectfully.

• Students have a class meeting to discuss how they have grown as readers and as members of a classroom community.

DO AHEAD

• Prior to Day 1, decide how you will randomly assign partners to work together during the unit.

• Prior to Day 1, have each student select a favorite book to recommend for summer reading (see Day 1, Steps 3–5, on pages 463–464).

• Prepare to model a book recommendation (see Day 1, Step 2, on page 463).

• Make copies of the Unit 9 Parent Letter (BLM23) to send home with the students on the last day of the unit.

Making Meaning Vocabulary Teacher

If you are teaching Developmental Studies Center's *Making Meaning Vocabulary* program, teach Vocabulary Week 25 this week. For more information, see the *Making Meaning Vocabulary Teacher's Manual*.

Day 1

Materials

- Book for modeling a recommendation (see Step 2)
- Students' books to recommend for summer reading (see "Do Ahead")
- "Self-monitoring Questions" chart

Being a Writer™ **Teacher**

You can either have the students work with their *Being a Writer* partner or assign them a different partner for the *Making Meaning* lessons.

Teacher Note

The book you choose for modeling making a book recommendation (see Step 2) could be a *Making Meaning* book that the students liked when you read it earlier this year, another popular book on the *Making Meaning* alternative book lists that you read aloud, or a book the students have not heard before. You might also want to collect other books to read aloud for the Extensions on Days 1 and 2.

Guided Strategy Practice

In this lesson, the students:

- Begin working with new partners
- Prepare to recommend a book for summer reading
- Read independently for up to 30 minutes

▶1 Pair Students and Get Ready to Work Together

Randomly assign partners and have them sit together. Tell them that during this last week of the *Making Meaning* program they will review the comprehension strategies they have learned, think about how they have grown as readers and as a community, share their favorite books, and plan their summer reading.

Tell them that at the end of this week they will also be asked to list some things they really enjoyed about working with partners this year. Encourage them to focus during the coming week on enjoying their partner work and using the skills they have learned to help them in their work together.

Confirm that each student has selected a book to recommend to others for summer reading. Explain that today they will discuss how to make summer reading book recommendations to their classmates. They will use the books they chose and will find an interesting short passage to read to the class. Tell the students you will use one of your favorite books to model ways to share a book with others.

Model a Book Recommendation

Model recommending a book to the class by briefly summarizing the book, saying what you liked about it, and reading a short passage aloud. Show the cover and read the title, author, and illustrator. (For example, you might say, "The book I want to recommend for your summer reading is *Stuart Little,* by E.B. White, illustrated by Garth Williams. It's a story about a mouse named Stuart who leaves home to find his best friend, Margalo, a bird who has mysteriously disappeared from her nest. Stuart has many exciting and humorous adventures as he looks for Margalo. I would recommend the book because Stuart is a funny character, and he goes from one wild adventure to another.")

Discuss What to Share in a Book Recommendation

Explain that the students will have some time now to plan what they want to say to their classmates about the books they chose. They will also choose a short passage from the book to read aloud. Ask:

Q *What information might be important to share when you recommend your book? Why?*

Q *What might be important to include when you tell what your book is about?*

Q *What might you want to look for in a passage to read aloud to the class?*

Students might say:

"It is important to share what the book is about."

"It is important to include the important ideas, but you don't want to tell the whole story."

"I want to read an exciting or interesting part. This way people might want to read the book."

Prepare to Share a Book Recommendation

Distribute the books that the students selected prior to this lesson. Have the students use their books to plan what they will say about them and to identify the passage they will read aloud. If it will be helpful, have the students quietly practice reading their passage aloud before sharing as a class.

Teacher Note

As the students prepare their book recommendations, circulate among them. Encourage them in their preparations by asking questions such as:

◀

Q *What passage are you planning to read? Why did you choose that passage?*

Q *How are you going to summarize the book?*

Q *What did you especially like about this book?*

5 ▶ Discuss Book Recommendations in Pairs

Have partners share their book recommendations and passages with each other and discuss the following questions. Write the questions where everyone can see them:

- *Does the recommendation summarize the book?*

- *Does the recommendation give just enough information?*

- *Does the recommendation make you want to read the book?*

- *Does the passage intrigue you and spark your interest?*

6 ▶ Discuss Working Together

When partners have discussed their book recommendations, bring the attention back to the whole class and ask:

Q *What did your partner do that was helpful?*

Q *How did you and your partner give each other feedback in a caring way? How did that help you?*

Explain that the students will have an opportunity in the coming days to share their book recommendations with the whole class.

INDIVIDUALIZED DAILY READING

7 ▶ Review and Discuss Self-monitoring

Direct the students' attention to the "Self-monitoring Questions" chart and remind them that a comprehension technique they learned this year is to stop and think about what they are reading and ask themselves questions to help them track their understanding. Tell them that they will practice this self-monitoring technique today during independent reading.

Have the students read independently for up to 30 minutes. Stop them at 10-minute intervals and have them monitor their comprehension by thinking about the charted questions.

Self-monitoring Questions

- *What is happening in my story right now?*

- *Does the reading make sense?*

At the end of independent reading, facilitate a whole-class discussion about how self-monitoring helps the students track their understanding.

Discuss questions such as:

Q *How does stopping and checking your understanding help you?*

Q *What are some things you do when you do not understand?*

EXTENSION

Introduce a Second Summer Reading Book Recommendation and Read Aloud

Tell the students that you will make another summer reading book recommendation by first summarizing the book and then reading the book aloud. Refer to the "Reading Comprehension Strategies" chart and remind the students to think about the comprehension strategies they are using as they listen.

Introduce the book by reading the information on the cover and providing any necessary background information and a brief summary. Read the book aloud, showing the illustrations. You might stop periodically to have partners discuss what they have heard so far.

Discuss the reading as a class. Have the students use "Turn to Your Partner" as appropriate to encourage thinking and participation. Be ready to reread passages to help the students recall what they heard. Ask questions such as:

Q *What is the story about?*

Q *What do you want to add to the summary [Sylvio] just gave?*

Q *Is this a book you would recommend to someone? Why or why not?*

Q *What comprehension strategies did you use as you listened to this story? How did that help you?*

Day 2

Materials

- Students' books to recommend for summer reading
- *Student Response Book* page 68

Guided Strategy Practice

In this lesson, the students:

- Begin their summer reading list
- Recommend books for summer reading
- Make choices about books they want to read
- Read independently for up to 30 minutes
- Discuss opinions respectfully

 Introduce the "Summer Reading List"

Confirm that each student has selected a book to recommend for summer reading. Explain that today the students will begin to share their book recommendations with the class. Tell them that they will have the opportunity to share their books over the next two days.

Have the students turn to *Student Response Book* page 68, "Summer Reading List." Explain that as they hear book recommendations in the coming days, they will list the books they might be interested in reading this summer. Point out that the "Summer Reading List" has space for the book title, author, and a few words to remind them about the book.

Remind the students that yesterday you recommended a book for their summer reading. Invite the students to add that book to their summer reading list if they wish. Write the title and author on the board so that interested students can copy the information.

 Review What to Share in a Book Recommendation

Briefly review sharing book recommendations by discussing questions such as:

Q *What might be important to include when you tell what your book is about?*

Q *What is important to remember when reading your passage aloud?*

 Share Book Recommendations

Call on a volunteer to share her book recommendation with the class. Remind the student to show the cover and read the title and the names of the author and illustrator before telling about the book and reading the selected passage to the class.

When the student has finished, facilitate a brief class discussion using questions such as:

Q *What questions do you want to ask [Krista] about the book she shared?*

Q *What did you hear about this book or in the passage that especially interested you?*

Q *[Krista], what were you thinking when you chose that passage?*

Q *Do you have enough information to decide whether you want to add this book to your summer reading list? If not, what else do you want to know?*

Ask the student who shared the book to write the book's title and author clearly on the board. Have the students copy this information onto their summer reading list if they are interested in reading the book over the summer.

Have several more students share their books and passages with the class. After each student shares, allow time for questions and discussion and for interested students to add to their reading list.

 Discuss Working Together

Have the students who shared their recommendations today talk briefly about how they felt the class treated them while they were sharing. Ask:

Q *What made you feel like your classmates were interested in what you were sharing?*

Q *If you weren't sure that your classmates were interested, what made you unsure?*

Open the discussion to the whole class, and ask:

Q *What should we do the same way, or differently, as we continue to share our book recommendations?*

Remind the students of your expectation that they will do their part to help create a safe, caring community in the class. Tell them that more students will share their book recommendations in the next lesson.

INDIVIDUALIZED DAILY READING

5 ▶ **Read Independently and Discuss Reading Comprehension Strategies**

Have the students read independently for up to 30 minutes.

As the students read, circulate among them. Ask individual students questions such as:

Q *What is this passage about?*

Q *What comprehension strategies are you using to help you understand what you are reading? Tell me what you thought about when you used that strategy.*

You might need to encourage the students' thinking with questions such as:

Q *What are some questions that come to your mind about what you are reading?*

Q *Have any pictures come to your mind about the reading? If so, what have you visualized? What helped bring this picture to your mind?*

Q *What do you think is an important idea in this story?*

At the end of independent reading, have the students verbally summarize for their partners what they read and talk about a reading comprehension strategy they used. As the students share, circulate and listen, observing the students' behaviors and responses.

EXTENSION

Introduce a Third Summer Reading Book Recommendation and Read Aloud

Tell the students that you will make another summer reading book recommendation by first summarizing the book and then reading the book aloud. Refer to the "Reading Comprehension Strategies" chart and remind the students to think about the comprehension strategies they are using as they listen.

Introduce the book by reading the information on the cover and providing any necessary background information and a brief summary. Read the book aloud, showing the illustrations. You might stop periodically to have partners discuss what they have heard so far.

Discuss the reading as a class. Use "Turn to Your Partner" as appropriate to encourage thinking and participation. Be ready to reread passages to help the students recall what they heard. Ask questions such as:

Q *What is the story about?*

Q *What do you want to add to the summary [Sonya] just gave?*

Q *Is this a book you would recommend to someone? Why or why not?*

Q *What comprehension strategy or strategies did you use as you listened to this story? How did that help you?*

Day 3

Materials

- Students' books to recommend for summer reading
- *Student Response Book* page 69

Guided Strategy Practice and Reflection

In this lesson, the students:

- Recommend books for summer reading
- Make choices about books they want to read
- Think and write about how they have grown as readers
- Read independently for up to 30 minutes
- Discuss opinions respectfully

1 Discuss Sharing Ideas Respectfully

Remind the students that in the previous lesson they began to share book recommendations for summer reading. They will hear several more book recommendations today and consider these books for their summer reading list. Explain that they will also spend some time reflecting on and writing about their own reading lives.

Discuss how the students will interact kindly and respectfully during today's sharing. Ask:

Q *How do you want your classmates to respond to your book recommendation, whether or not they would choose to read your book? Why?*

Q *How can you let your classmates know that you are interested in the book they are sharing, and that you appreciate the work they've done to share it with you?*

Encourage them to keep these things in mind as they participate today.

Continue to Share Book Recommendations

Have several more students share their books and passages with the class. Remind them to begin by showing the cover of their book and reading the title and the name of the author aloud.

Facilitate a brief class discussion after each student shares, and have the student write the book's title and author on the board for interested students to copy. Use questions such as:

Q *What questions do you want to ask [Tim] about the book [he] shared?*

Q *What did you hear about the book or in the passage that especially interested you?*

Q *[Tim], what were you thinking when you chose that passage?*

Q *Do you have enough information to decide whether you want to add this book to your summer reading list? If not, what else do you want to know?*

After several students have shared their book recommendation, end the sharing time for today and tell the class that the remaining students will share their book recommendations tomorrow. Ask:

Q *If you hear about a book you are interested in reading, how might you find that book this summer to read?*

> **Students might say:**
>
> "I might find the book at the public library."
>
> "If a friend has the book, I could borrow it from her."
>
> "I might look for it at the bookstore, or on the Internet."

If the students have difficulty answering this question, suggest some ideas like those in the "Students might say" note.

Teacher Note

If not all the students are able to share their book recommendations, make time later in the day or on another day for them to share before proceeding with the Day 4 lesson.

Teacher Note

You might consider taking your students on a short field trip to a local library.

3 ▶ Reflect on Our Reading Lives

Explain that the students will now have a chance to think about how they have grown and changed as readers over the year. Remind them that they started the year thinking about their reading lives, and tell them that they will think about this again now that they are nearing the end of the year.

Ask the students to close their eyes and think quietly as you pose the following questions. Give them time to think between the questions:

Q *What are some of your favorite books now? Why?*

Q *Where is your favorite place to read?*

Q *What does the word* reading *mean to you?*

Q *When you don't understand something you are reading, what do you do?*

Q *What kinds of books did you read for the first time this year? What topics did you read about for the first time?*

Ask the students to turn to "Thoughts About My Reading Life" on *Student Response Book* page 69. Have them record some of the answers to these questions.

Tell them that they will share some of their thoughts during a class meeting tomorrow.

INDIVIDUALIZED DAILY READING

4 ▶ Read Independently and Discuss Reading Comprehension Strategies

Have the students read independently for up to 30 minutes.

As the students read, circulate among them. Ask individual students questions such as:

Q *What is this passage about?*

Q *What comprehension strategies are you using to help you understand what you are reading? Tell me what you thought about when you used that strategy.*

You might need to encourage the students' thinking with questions such as:

Q *What are some questions that come to your mind about what you are reading?*

Q *Have any pictures come to your mind about the reading? If so, what have you visualized? What helped bring this picture to your mind?*

Q *What do you think is an important idea in this story?*

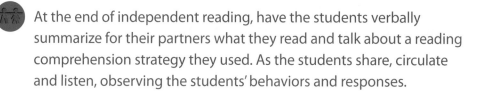 At the end of independent reading, have the students verbally summarize for their partners what they read and talk about a reading comprehension strategy they used. As the students share, circulate and listen, observing the students' behaviors and responses.

EXTENSION

Review the Summer Reading Lists

Have the students review the books on their summer reading lists. Ask:

Q *What kinds of books did you choose for summer reading? Does that surprise you? Why or why not?*

You might ask the students to put a star next to the books they want to read first. Encourage them to read as many of the books on their list as they can this summer. Also encourage them to talk with family members and friends about the books they are reading and to add any interesting books to their reading list.

Day 4

Materials

- Space for the class to sit in a circle
- "Class Meeting Ground Rules" chart
- *Student Response Book* page 70
- *Assessment Resource Book*
- Small self-stick notes for each student
- *Student Response Book,* IDR Journal section
- Unit 9 Parent Letter (BLM23)

Reflection and Class Meeting

In this lesson, the students:

- Think and write about how they have grown as members of the classroom community
- Have a class meeting to discuss how they have grown as readers and as members of a classroom community
- Read independently for up to 30 minutes

1 ▶ Reflect on Our Classroom Community

Remind the students that yesterday they reflected on and wrote about their growth as readers. Explain that the students will now have a chance to think about how they did creating a safe and caring community this year and how they personally have changed as members of the community. Tell the students that later they will have a chance to share their thoughts about how they have grown as readers and as members of a classroom community during a class meeting.

Use "Think, Pair, Share" to have the students think about and discuss the following questions. After asking each question, have the students close their eyes. Give them a few seconds to think quietly before signaling them to talk in pairs.

Q *Think about how you worked with your first partner this year. Think about how you are working with your partner now. How have you grown in your ability to work with a partner?*

Q *How have we done at becoming a caring and safe community this year? What makes you think so?*

Q *How has being part of this community helped you this year?*

Q *What three things did you like most about working with partners?*

After the students have discussed the questions, ask them to turn to "Thoughts About Our Classroom Community" on *Student Response Book* page 70. Have them record their answers for these questions.

2 Gather for a Class Meeting

Review the procedure for coming to a class meeting and have the students move to the circle with their *Student Response Books* and with partners sitting together. Explain that during the first part of the class meeting they will discuss how they have grown as readers and during the second part of the class meeting they will talk about their classroom community and what they enjoyed about working with a partner.

Make sure the students can see all their classmates, and briefly review the "Class Meeting Ground Rules" chart.

3 Discuss Growth as Readers

Remind the students that one of the ways they built their reading community this year was to share their reading lives with one another. Explain that one of the purposes of this class meeting is to talk about ways they have changed and grown as readers. Facilitate a discussion using questions such as:

Q *How do you think you have changed or grown as a reader? What makes you think that?*

Q *Do others think they have changed or grown in a similar way? Why do you think so?*

Q *In what ways are you the same kind of reader as you were at the beginning of the year?*

Q *What questions do you want to ask [Jena] about what [she] said?*

Have the students use "Turn to Your Partner" as needed during this discussion to increase accountability and participation.

> **Teacher Note**
>
> You may want to hold the class meeting later in the day or on the following day.

> *Class Meeting Ground Rules*
>
> - one person talks at a time
> - listen to one another

Students might say:

"My favorite books used to be the books about Ramona. I still like those books, but my new favorite books are mysteries."

"At the beginning of the year, I wrote 'I don't know' for the question '*When you don't understand something you are reading, what do you do?*' At the end of the year, I wrote, 'I ask myself questions, and then I read it again.'"

"In September, I wrote that I wanted to read about space this year, and I did. I read a bunch of books about the solar system."

"I used to think reading meant reading words. Now I think reading means thinking about a story."

You might want to share some of your general observations about ways your students have changed or grown as readers over the year. (For example, you might say, "I noticed that all of you have improved in your ability to choose books that are at the right reading level for you and that you are choosing books now that are at a higher reading level than those you chose at the beginning of the year.")

4 ▶ Discuss Our Community and Partner Work

Explain that the second purpose of this class meeting is to talk about the classroom community and for students to share some of their favorite things about working with a partner this year. Facilitate a discussion using questions such as:

Q *How did we do creating the kind of classroom we wanted this year? What makes you think so?*

Q *How has being part of this community helped you this year?*

Q *What are three things that you liked most about working with partners this year?*

Students might say:

"At first it was hard, but we got better and better at it."

"I think the more we got to know each other, the more we were a community."

"I agree with [Celeste]. Being in this community has helped me because I used to be too shy to say anything to the class. I don't feel that way anymore."

"In addition to what [Raymond] said, I liked working with a partner. I liked having someone to talk to, not having to be quiet all the time, and getting to work with different partners."

You might want to share some of your general observations about ways your students have changed or grown as members of the community over the year. (For example, you might say, "I remember how some students didn't want to work with an assigned partner at the beginning of the year. Now you are much better at working with any partner. I also noticed that you relied much more heavily on me at the beginning of the year to help you solve your problems. Now you are able to solve many problems by yourselves.") Ask:

Q *What is one thing you learned about working well with a partner that you want to take with you next year?*

▶5 **Reflect and Adjourn the Class Meeting**

Briefly discuss how the students did following the ground rules during the class meeting, and adjourn the meeting.

INDIVIDUALIZED DAILY READING

▶6 **Write About Reading Comprehension Strategies in Their IDR Journals**

Have the students read independently for up to 30 minutes, using self-stick notes to mark places where they notice they are using a reading comprehension strategy.

As the students read, circulate among them. Ask individual students questions such as:

Q *What is your reading about?*

Q *I notice that you placed a self-stick note in this part of your book. What comprehension strategy helped you understand this part?*

FACILITATION TIP

Reflect on your experience over the past year using the facilitation tips included in the *Making Meaning* program. Did using the facilitation techniques feel natural to you? Have you integrated them into your class discussions throughout the school day? What effect did using the facilitation techniques have on your students? We encourage you to continue to use the facilitation techniques and reflect on students' responses as you facilitate class discussions in the future.

At the end of independent reading, have each student summarize her reading and write about a comprehension strategy she used—the name of the strategy and where she used it—in her IDR Journal.

SOCIAL SKILLS ASSESSMENT

Take this opportunity to reflect on your students' social development over the year. Review the Social Skills Assessment record sheet on pages 2–3 of the *Assessment Resource Book* and note student growth. Use this information to help you plan for next year. Ask yourself questions such as:

Q *What was challenging for my students this year in terms of their social development?*

Q *How might I help next year's students grow socially?*

Q *What skills should I emphasize with the students next year to help them build a safe and caring reading community?*

EXTENSION

End-of-year "Summer Reading Fair"

Have the students invite other second- or third-grade classes to a "Summer Reading Fair." Have the students present their books to small groups of students. The invited students will have an opportunity to listen to the students talk about their favorite books, preview the books, and get a glimpse of the reading life of the students. Students might also make posters to advertise their favorite books. If there is a school library or librarian available, you might want to involve the library in the activity.

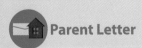

Parent Letter

Send home with each student the Parent Letter for this unit (see "Do Ahead," p. 461).

Appendices

Grade 3

	Lesson	Title	Author	Form	Genre/Type
Unit 1	▶ Week 1	*Miss Nelson Is Missing!*	Harry Allard	picture book	fiction
		Officer Buckle and Gloria	Peggy Rathmann	picture book	fiction
	▶ Week 2	*The Man Who Walked Between the Towers*	Mordicai Gerstein	picture book	narrative nonfiction
Unit 2	▶ Week 1	*Have You Seen Bugs?*	Joanne Oppenheim	picture book	narrative nonfiction
		Cherries and Cherry Pits	Vera B. Williams	picture book	realistic fiction
	▶ Week 2	*The Spooky Tail of Prewitt Peacock*	Bill Peet	picture book	fiction
	▶ Week 3	*Aunt Flossie's Hats (and Crab Cakes Later)*	Elizabeth Fitzgerald Howard	picture book	realistic fiction
Unit 3	▶ Week 1	*The Paper Bag Princess*	Robert Munsch	picture book	fiction
	▶ Week 2	*Julius, the Baby of the World*	Kevin Henkes	picture book	fiction
	▶ Week 3	*Boundless Grace*	Mary Hoffman	picture book	realistic fiction
	▶ Week 4	*City Green*	DyAnne DiSalvo-Ryan	picture book	realistic fiction
	▶ Week 5	*Alexander, Who's Not (Do you hear me? I mean it!) Going to Move*	Judith Viorst	picture book	realistic fiction
Unit 4	▶ Week 1	*The Girl Who Loved Wild Horses*	Paul Goble	picture book	fiction
		Knots on a Counting Rope	Bill Martin Jr. and John Archambault	picture book	realistic fiction
	▶ Week 2	*A Day's Work*	Eve Bunting	picture book	realistic fiction
	▶ Week 3	*Mailing May*	Michael O. Tunnell	picture book	historical fiction
	▶ Week 4	*Brave Irene*	William Steig	picture book	fiction
Unit 5	▶ Week 1	*Brave Harriet*	Marissa Moss	picture book	narrative nonfiction
	▶ Week 2	*Wilma Unlimited*	Kathleen Krull	picture book	narrative nonfiction
Unit 6	▶ Week 1	*Morning Meals Around the World*	Maryellen Gregoire	picture book	expository nonfiction
	▶ Week 2	*Reptiles*	Melissa Stewart	picture book	expository nonfiction
	▶ Week 3	"Hop to It"		article	expository nonfiction
		"Origami"		article	expository nonfiction
		"How to Make a Paper Airplane"		functional text	expository nonfiction
		"Lincoln School Lunch Calendar for the week of May 21–May 25"		functional text	expository nonfiction
Unit 7	▶ Week 1	*Flashy Fantastic Rain Forest Frogs*	Dorothy Hinshaw Patent	picture book	expository nonfiction
	▶ Week 2	*What Is a Bat?*	Bobbie Kalman and Heather Levigne	picture book	expository nonfiction
	▶ Week 3	"Why Do Animals Play?"	Kathleen Weidner Zoehfeld	article	expository nonfiction
		"Feeling the Heat"	Kathryn R. Satterfield	article	expository nonfiction
		"Banning Tag"		article	expository nonfiction
Unit 8	▶ Week 1	*Fables*	Arnold Lobel	picture book	fiction
	▶ Week 2	*Lifetimes*	David L. Rice	picture book	expository nonfiction
		A Day's Work	Eve Bunting	picture book	realistic fiction
	▶ Week 3	*Keepers*	Jeri Hanel Watts	picture book	realistic fiction
Unit 9	▶ Week 1	Student-selected book			

Grade K

Brave Bear	Kathy Mallat
Building Beavers	Kathleen Martin-James
Cat's Colors	Jane Cabrera
"Charlie Needs a Cloak"	Tomie dePaola
Cookie's Week	Cindy Ward
A Day with a Doctor	Jan Kottke
A Day with a Mail Carrier	Jan Kottke
Flower Garden	Eve Bunting
Friends at School	Rochelle Bunnett
Getting Around By Plane	Cassie Mayer
Henry's Wrong Turn	Harriet M. Ziefert
I Want to Be a Vet	Dan Liebman
I Was So Mad	Mercer Mayer
If You Give a Mouse a Cookie	Laura Joffe Numeroff
Knowing about Noses	Allan Fowler
A Letter to Amy	Ezra Jack Keats
Maisy's Pool	Lucy Cousins
Moon	Melanie Mitchell
My Friends	Taro Gomi
Noisy Nora	Rosemary Wells
On the Go	Ann Morris
A Porcupine Named Fluffy	Helen Lester
Pumpkin Pumpkin	Jeanne Titherington
A Tiger Cub Grows Up	Joan Hewett
Tools	Ann Morris
When Sophie Gets Angry— Really, Really Angry…	Molly Bang
Whistle for Willie	Ezra Jack Keats

Grade 1

Caps for Sale	Esphyr Slobodkina
Chrysanthemum	Kevin Henkes
Curious George Goes to an Ice Cream Shop	Margret Rey and Alan J. Shalleck (editors)
A Day in the Life of a Garbage Collector	Nate LeBoutillier
Did You See What I Saw? Poems about School	Kay Winters
Dinosaur Babies	Lucille Recht Penner
Down the Road	Alice Schertle
An Elephant Grows Up	Anastasia Suen
An Extraordinary Egg	Leo Lionni
George Washington and the General's Dog	Frank Murphy
A Good Night's Sleep	Allan Fowler
A Harbor Seal Pup Grows Up	Joan Hewett
Hearing	Sharon Gordon
In the Tall, Tall Grass	Denise Fleming
It's Mine!	Leo Lionni
Julius	Angela Johnson
A Kangaroo Joey Grows Up	Joan Hewett
A Look at Teeth	Allan Fowler
Matthew and Tilly	Rebecca C. Jones
McDuff and the Baby	Rosemary Wells
Peter's Chair	Ezra Jack Keats
Quick as a Cricket	Audrey Wood
Raptors!	Lisa McCourt
Sheep Out to Eat	Nancy Shaw
The Snowy Day	Ezra Jack Keats
Throw Your Tooth on the Roof	Selby B. Beeler
When I Was Little	Jamie Lee Curtis
Where Do I Live?	Neil Chesanow

Grade 2

Alexander and the Terrible, Horrible, No Good, Very Bad Day	Judith Viorst
The Art Lesson	Tomie dePaola
Beatrix Potter	Alexandra Wallner
Bend and Stretch	Pamela Hill Nettleton
Big Al	Andrew Clements
Chester's Way	Kevin Henkes
Eat My Dust! Henry Ford's First Race	Monica Kulling
Erandi's Braids	Antonio Hernández Madrigal
Fathers, Mothers, Sisters, Brothers: A Collection of Family Poems	Mary Ann Hoberman
Fishes (A True Book)	Melissa Stewart
Galimoto	Karen Lynn Williams
The Ghost-Eye Tree	Bill Martin Jr. and John Archambault
The Incredible Painting of Felix Clousseau	Jon Agee
It Could Still Be a Worm	Allan Fowler
Jamaica Tag-Along	Juanita Havill
little blue and little yellow	Leo Lionni
McDuff Moves In	Rosemary Wells
Me First	Helen Lester
The Paper Crane	Molly Bang
The Paperboy	Dav Pilkey
Plants That Eat Animals	Allan Fowler
POP! A Book About Bubbles	Kimberly Brubaker Bradley
Poppleton	Cynthia Rylant
Poppleton and Friends	Cynthia Rylant
Sheila Rae, the Brave	Kevin Henkes
Snails	Monica Hughes
The Tale of Peter Rabbit	Beatrix Potter
A Tree Is Nice	Janice May Udry
What Mary Jo Shared	Janice May Udry

Grade 4

Amelia's Road	Linda Jacobs Altman
Animal Senses	Pamela Hickman
A Bad Case of Stripes	David Shannon
Basket Moon	Mary Lyn Ray
The Bat Boy & His Violin	Gavin Curtis
Chicken Sunday	Patricia Polacco
Coming to America	Betsy Maestro
Digging Up Tyrannosaurus Rex	John R. Horner and Don Lessem
Farm Workers Unite: The Great Grape Boycott	
Flight	Robert Burleigh
Hurricane	David Wiesner
In My Own Backyard	Judi Kurjian
Italian Americans	Carolyn P. Yoder
My Man Blue	Nikki Grimes
The Old Woman Who Named Things	Cynthia Rylant
Peppe the Lamplighter	Elisa Bartone
A Picture Book of Amelia Earhart	David A. Adler
A Picture Book of Harriet Tubman	David A. Adler
A Picture Book of Rosa Parks	David A. Adler
The Princess and the Pizza	Mary Jane and Herm Auch
Slinky Scaly Slithery Snakes	Dorothy Hinshaw Patent
Song and Dance Man	Karen Ackerman
Teammates	Peter Golenbock
Thunder Cake	Patricia Polacco

Grade 5

Big Cats	Seymour Simon
Chinese Americans	Tristan Boyer Binns
Earthquakes	Seymour Simon
Everybody Cooks Rice	Norah Dooley
Harry Houdini: Master of Magic	Robert Kraske
Heroes	Paul Dowswell
Hey World, Here I Am!	Jean Little
Letting Swift River Go	Jane Yolen
Life in the Rain Forests	Lucy Baker
The Lotus Seed	Sherry Garland
Richard Wright and the Library Card	William Miller
A River Ran Wild	Lynne Cherry
Something to Remember Me By	Susan V. Bosak
Star of Fear, Star of Hope	Jo Hoestlandt
The Summer My Father Was Ten	Pat Brisson
Survival and Loss: Native American Boarding Schools	
Uncle Jed's Barbershop	Margaree King Mitchell
The Van Gogh Cafe	Cynthia Rylant
Wildfires	Seymour Simon

Grade 6

America Street: A Multicultural Anthology of Stories	Anne Mazer, ed.
And Still the Turtle Watched	Sheila MacGill-Callahan
Asian Indian Americans	Carolyn P. Yoder
Baseball Saved Us	Ken Mochizuki
Chato's Kitchen	Gary Soto
Dear Benjamin Banneker	Andrea Davis Pinkney
Encounter	Jane Yolen
Every Living Thing	Cynthia Rylant
Life in the Oceans	Lucy Baker
New Kids in Town: Oral Histories of Immigrant Teens	Janet Bode
Out of This World: Science Fiction Stories	Edward Blishen, ed.
Rosie the Riveter: Women in a Time of War	
The Strangest of Strange Unsolved Mysteries, Volume 2	Phyllis Raybin Emert
Train to Somewhere	Eve Bunting
Voices from the Fields	S. Beth Atkin
Volcano: The Eruption and Healing of Mount St. Helens	Patricia Lauber
Whales	Seymour Simon
Why Mosquitoes Buzz in People's Ears	Verna Aardema

Grade 7

Ancient Ones: The World of the Old-Growth Douglas Fir	Barbara Bash
Children of the Wild West	Russell Freedman
Death of the Iron Horse	Paul Goble
The Dream Keeper and Other Poems	Langston Hughes
Finding Our Way	René Saldaña, Jr.
the flag of childhood: poems from the middle east	Naomi Shahib Nye, ed.
The Friendship	Mildred D. Taylor
It's Our World, Too!	Phillip Hoose
The Land I Lost	Huynh Quang Nhuong
Life in the Woodlands	Roseanne Hooper
New and Selected Poems	Gary Soto
Only Passing Through: The Story of Sojourner Truth	Anne Rockwell
Roberto Clemente: Pride of the Pittsburgh Pirates	Jonah Winter
Shattered: Stories of Children and War	Jennifer Armstrong, ed.
Sports Stories	Alan Durant, ed.
The Village That Vanished	Ann Grifalconi
What If…? Amazing Stories	Monica Hughes, ed.
Wolves	Seymour Simon
The Wretched Stone	Chris Van Allsburg

Grade 8

the composition	Antonio Skármeta
The Giver	Lois Lowry
Immigrant Kids	Russell Freedman
In the Land of the Lawn Weenies	David Lubar
Life in the Polar Lands	Monica Byles
Nellie Bly: A Name to Be Reckoned With	Stephen Krensky
The People Could Fly	Virginia Hamilton
Satchel Paige	Lesa Cline-Ransome
Sharks	Seymour Simon
She Dared: True Stories of Heroines, Scoundrels, and Renegades	Ed Butts
When I Was Your Age: Original Stories About Growing Up, Volume One	Amy Ehrlich, ed.

Bibliography

Anderson, Richard C., Elfrieda H. Hiebert, Judith A. Scott, and Ian A. G. Wilkinson. *Becoming a Nation of Readers: The Report of the Commission on Reading*. Washington, DC: The National Institute of Education, 1985.

Anderson, Richard C., and P. David Pearson. "A Schema-Theoretic View of Basic Process in Reading Comprehension." In *Handbook of Reading Research*, P. David Pearson (ed.). New York: Longman, 1984.

Armbruster, Bonnie B., Fred Lehr, and Jean Osborn. *Put Reading First: The Research Building Blocks for Teaching Children to Read*. Jessup, MD: National Institute for Literacy, 2001.

Asher, James. "The Strategy of Total Physical Response: An Application to Learning Russian." *International Review of Applied Linguistics* 3 (1965): 291–300.

———. "Children's First Language as a Model for Second Language Learning." *Modern Language Journal* 56 (1972): 133–139.

Beck, Isabel L., and Margaret G. McKeown. "Text Talk: Capturing the Benefits of Read-Aloud Experiences for Young Children." *The Reading Teacher* 55:1 (2001): 10–19.

Beck, Isabel L., Margaret G. McKeown, and Linda Kucan. *Bringing Words to Life: Robust Vocabulary Instruction*. New York: Guilford Press (2002).

Block, C. C., and M. Pressley. *Comprehension Instruction: Research-Based Best Practices*. New York: Guilford Press, 2001.

Calkins, Lucy M. *The Art of Teaching Reading*. New York: Addison-Wesley Longman, 2001.

Contestable, Julie W., Shaila Regan, Susie Alldredge, Carol Westrich, and Laurel Robertson. *Number Power: A Cooperative Approach to Mathematics and Social Development Grades K–6*. Oakland, CA: Developmental Studies Center, 1999.

Cummins, James. "The Role of Primary Language Development in Promoting Educational Success for Language Minority Students." In *Schooling and Language Minority Students: A Theoretical Framework*. Los Angeles, CA: California State University, Evaluation, Dissemination, and Assessment Center, 1981.

Cunningham, Anne E., and Keith E. Stanovich. "What Reading Does for the Mind." *American Educator* Spring/Summer (1998): 8–15.

Developmental Studies Center. *Blueprints for a Collaborative Classroom*. Oakland, CA: Developmental Studies Center, 1997.

———. *Ways We Want Our Class to Be*. Oakland, CA: Developmental Studies Center, 1996.

DeVries, Rheta, and Betty Zan. *Moral Classrooms, Moral Children*. New York: Teachers' College Press, 1994.

Dewey, J. *Democracy and Education*. New York: Macmillan, 1916.

Farstrup, Alan E., and S. Jay Samuels. *What Research Has to Say About Reading Instruction*. 3rd Ed. Newark, DE: International Reading Association, 2002.

Fielding, Linda G., and P. David Pearson. "Reading Comprehension: What Works." *Educational Leadership* 51:5 (1994): 1–11.

Fountas, Irene C. and Gay Su Pinnell. *Leveled Books, K–8: Matching Texts to Readers for Effective Teaching*. Portsmouth, NH: Heinemann, 2006.

———. *Leveled Books for Readers Grade 3–6*. Portsmouth, NH: Heinemann, 2002.

———. *Matching Books to Readers: Using Leveled Books in Guided Reading, K–3*. Portsmouth, NH: Heinemann, 1999.

Gambrell, Linda B., Lesley Mandel Morrow, Susan B. Neuman, and Michael Pressley, eds. *Best Practices in Literacy Instruction*. New York: Guilford Press, 1999.

Hakuta, Kenji, Yoko Goto Butler, and Daria Witt. *How Long Does It Take English Learners to Attain Proficiency?* Santa Barbara, CA: University of California, Linguistic Minority Research Institute, 2000.

Harvey, Stephanie. *Nonfiction Matters: Reading, Writing, and Research in Grades 3–8*. York, ME: Stenhouse Publishers, 1998.

Harvey, Stephanie, and Anne Goudvis. *Strategies That Work: Teaching Comprehension to Enhance Understanding*. York, ME: Stenhouse Publishers, 2000.

Harvey, Stephanie, Sheila McAuliffe, Laura Benson, Wendy Cameron, Sue Kempton, Pat Lusche, Debbie Miller, Joan Schroeder, and Julie Weaver. "Teacher-Researchers Study the Process of Synthesizing in Six Primary Classrooms." *Language Arts* 73 (1996): 564–574.

Herrell, Adrienne L. and Michael L. Jordan. *Fifty Strategies for Teaching English Language Learners*. Upper Saddle River, NJ: Merrill, 2000.

International Reading Association. "What Is Evidence-Based Reading Instruction? A Position Statement of the International Reading Association." Newark, DE: International Reading Association, 2002.

Johnson, David W., Roger T. Johnson, and Edythe Johnson Holubec. *The New Circles of Learning: Cooperation in the Classroom*. Alexandria, VA: Association for Supervision and Curriculum Development, 1994.

Kagan, Spencer. *Cooperative Learning*. San Juan Capistrano, CA: Resources of Teachers, 1992.

Kamil, Michael L., Peter B. Mosenthal, P. David Pearson, and Rebecca Barr, eds. *Handbook of Reading Research, Volume III*. Mahwah, NJ: Lawrence Erlbaum Associates, 2000.

Keene, Ellin O., and Susan Zimmermann. *Mosaic of Thought: Teaching Comprehension in a Reader's Workshop*. Portsmouth, NH: Heinemann, 1997.

Kohlberg, Lawrence. *The Psychology of Moral Development*. New York: Harper and Row, 1984.

Kohn, Alfie. *Beyond Discipline: From Compliance to Community*. Association for Supervision and Curriculum Development, 1996.

————. *Punished by Rewards: The Trouble with Gold Stars, Incentive Plans, A's, Praise, and Other Bribes*. New York: Houghton Mifflin Company, 1999.

Krashen, Stephen D. *Principles and Practice in Second Language Acquisition*. New York: Prentice-Hall, 1982.

Moss, Barbara. "Making a Case and a Place for Effective Content Area Literacy Instruction in the Elementary Grades." *The Reading Teacher* 59:1 (2005): 46–55.

NEA Task Force on Reading. *Report of the NEA Task Force on Reading 2000*.

Neufeld, Paul. "Comprehension Instruction in Content Area Classes." *The Reading Teacher* 59:4 (2005): 302–312.

Nucci, Larry P., ed. *Moral Development and Character Education: A Dialogue*. Berkeley, CA: McCutchan Publishing Corporation, 1989.

Optiz, Michael F., ed. *Literacy Instruction for Culturally and Linguistically Diverse Students*. Newark, DE: International Reading Association, 1998.

Pearson, P. David, J. A. Dole, G. G. Duffy, and L. R. Roehler. "Developing Expertise in Reading Comprehension: What Should Be Taught and How Should It Be Taught?" In *What Research Has to Say to the Teacher of Reading*, J. Farstup and S. J. Samuels (eds.). Newark, DE: International Reading Association, 1992.

Piaget, Jean. *The Child's Conception of the World*. Trans. Joan and Andrew Tomlinson. Lanham, MD: Littlefield Adams, 1969.

————. *The Moral Judgment of the Child*. Trans. Marjorie Gabain. New York: The Free Press, 1965.

Pressley, Michael. *Effective Beginning Reading Instruction: The Rest of the Story from Research*. National Education Association, 2002.

————. *Reading Instruction That Works*. New York: Guilford Press, 1998.

Pressley, Michael, Janice Almasi, Ted Schuder, Janet Bergman, Sheri Hite, Pamela B. El-Dinary, and Rachel Brown. "Transactional Instruction of Comprehension Strategies: The Montgomery County, Maryland, SAIL Program." *Reading and Writing Quarterly: Overcoming Learning Difficulties* 10 (1994): 5–19.

Routman, Regie. *Reading Essentials: The Specifics You Need to Teach Reading Well*. Portsmouth, NH: Heinemann, 2003.

Serafini, Frank. *The Reading Workshop: Creating Space for Readers*. Portsmouth, NH: Heinemann, 2001.

Soalt, Jennifer. "Bringing Together Fictional and Informational Texts to Improve Comprehension." *The Reading Teacher* 58:7 (2005): 680–683.

Taylor, Barbara M., Michael Pressley, and P. David Pearson. *Research-Supported Characteristics of Teachers and Schools That Promote Reading Achievement*. National Education Association, 2002.

Trelease, Jim. *The Read-Aloud Handbook*. New York: Penguin Books, 1995.

Weaver, Brenda M. *Leveling Books K–6: Matching Readers to Text*. Newark, DE: International Reading Association, 2000.

Williams, Joan A. "Classroom Conversations: Opportunities to Learn for ESL Students in Mainstream Classrooms." *The Reading Teacher* 54:8 (2001): 750–757.

Blackline Masters

Dear Parent or Guardian,

Our class just finished the fifth unit of the *Making Meaning*® program. During this unit, the students identified what they learned from nonfiction books. They also wondered and asked questions to help them make sense of what they read. *Wondering/questioning* helps readers understand all kinds of nonfiction materials, including biographies, magazines, textbooks, websites, encyclopedias, and other texts that give the reader true information. Socially, the students practiced contributing ideas that are different from others' ideas.

You can support what your child has been learning at school by reading nonfiction at home together. Discussing what you wonder and what questions you both have about what you are reading will help deepen your child's understanding. You might get your child to think about what he or she is wondering by asking questions about what you read together, such as:

- What do you wonder about this topic?

- What did you find out from the reading?

- What is one thing you learned that surprised you?

- After reading, what do you still wonder?

Talking about the books and articles you read together can help your child learn from and enjoy nonfiction. I hope you and your child continue to enjoy reading and learning together.

Sincerely,

Apreciado padre de familia o guardián:

Nuestra clase acaba de finalizar la quinta unidad del programa "*Making Meaning.®*" Durante esta unidad los estudiantes identificaron lo que aprendieron de los libros que no son ficción. Ellos también hicieron preguntas para ayudar a entender lo que leyeron.

El hacer preguntas ayuda a los lectores a entender toda clase de materiales que no son ficción incluyendo: biografías, revistas, libros de textos escolares, páginas del Internet, enciclopedias, y otros textos que le brindan al lector información verídica. Socialmente, los estudiantes practicaron al contribuir ideas que fueran distintas a las de otros.

Usted puede apoyar a lo que su niño ha aprendido en la escuela al leer juntos textos que no sean ficción en la casa. El hablar acerca de las preguntas que ambos tienen acerca de lo que están leyendo puede ayudarle a su niño a obtener un entendimiento más a fondo. Usted puede hacer que su niño se ponga a pensar en las preguntas que tiene en la mente al hacerle preguntas referentes a lo que leyeron juntos como:

- ¿Qué preguntas tienes acerca de este tema?

- ¿Qué descubriste al leer?

- ¿Cuál fue una cosa que aprendiste que te sorprendió?

- Después de haber leído, ¿qué preguntas tiene todavia?

El hablar acerca de los libros y los artículos que leyeron juntos, le puede ayudar a su niño aprender y a disfrutar de los textos de no ficción. Espero que usted y su niño continúen leyendo y aprendiendo juntos.

Sinceramente,

Dear Parent or Guardian,

Our class just finished the sixth unit of the *Making Meaning*® program. During this unit, the students read nonfiction books and articles about specific topics. They also examined functional texts, or nonfiction texts that help the reader do something, such as maps, instructions, or street signs. The students explored some of the features often found in nonfiction texts, such as tables of contents, indexes, headings, photos, maps, graphs, and diagrams.

You can support your child's reading life at home by:

- Collecting nonfiction that is interesting to your child.

- Talking about what you both learn from the nonfiction you read.

- Noticing and talking about functional texts you encounter throughout the day, such as nutrition labels, game schedules, or traffic signs.

Before reading nonfiction together, it can be helpful to ask your child:

- What do you think we will learn about this topic?

After reading nonfiction it can be helpful to ask:

- What did you find out about the topic?

- What is something you learned that surprised you?

- After reading this, what questions do you still have?

I hope you and your child enjoy learning together about topics of interest to both of you. Happy reading!

Sincerely,

Apreciado padre de familia o guardián:

Nuestra clase acaba de finalizar la sexta unidad del programa "*Making Meaning.*®" Durante esta unidad los estudiantes leyeron libros de no ficción y artículos de temas específicos. Los estudiantes exploraron algunos de los aspectos que frecuentemente se encuentran en los textos de no ficción, como lo son: índices, lista de contenido, encabezamientos, fotos, mapas, gráficos y diagramas. También examinaron textos funcionales como mapas, instrucciones, cuadros y señales de las calles.

En casa usted puede apoyar la lectura de su niño al hacer lo siguiente:

- Coleccionar textos de no ficción que sean de interés para su niño.

- Hablar acerca de lo que ambos aprendieron al leer juntos el texto de no ficción.

- Fijarse y hablar de los textos de no ficción durante el día, como cuando ven los rótulos del contenido nutricional, los horarios de juegos o señales de tráfico.

Puede ayudar a su niño si antes de empezar a leer juntos textos de no ficción, usted le pregunta:

- ¿Qué crees que vas a aprender acerca del tema?

Después de leer textos de no ficción, puede ayudar al hacer las siguientes preguntas:

- ¿Qué encontraste acerca del tema?

- ¿Qué aprendiste que te sorprendió?

- Después de haber leído esto, ¿cuáles son las preguntas que aún tienes?

Espero que el aprender juntos acerca de temas de mutuo interés sea divertido. ¡Feliz lectura!

Sinceramente,

Dear Parent or Guardian,

Our class just finished the seventh unit of the *Making Meaning*® program. During this unit, the students continued to hear and discuss nonfiction texts. They talked about what they learned from the nonfiction texts and articles, and asked questions about the topics they heard about during the read-alouds. *Wondering* or *asking questions* about a topic before, during, and after reading helps readers actively engage with the text and make sense of what they are reading.

You can support your child's reading life at home by collecting nonfiction texts that interest your child, and talking about what your child is learning from the nonfiction that you read aloud or that your child reads independently.

Before reading a nonfiction text to your child, it is helpful to ask questions such as:

- What do you think you know about [bats]?

- What questions do you have about [bats]?

Consider stopping every so often during the reading to ask what your child is learning and what questions he or she still has.

After reading, you might ask questions such as:

- What did you learn about [bats] from this book?

- What did you learn that surprised you?

- What are you still wondering about [bats]?

I hope you and your child continue to enjoy reading together. Happy reading!

Sincerely,

Apreciado padre de familia o guardián:

Nuestra clase acaba de finalizar la séptima unidad del programa "*Making Meaning.*®" Durante esta unidad los estudiantes siguieron escuchando y hablando acerca de textos de no ficción. Ellos hablaron acerca de lo que aprendieron de los textos y artículos de no ficción y formularon preguntas referentes a los temas que escucharon durante la sesión de lectura en voz alta. *El hacer preguntas* sobre una materia, antes, durante y después de la lectura, ayuda a que los lectores se involucren activamente con el texto y que entiendan lo que están leyendo.

Usted puede apoyar la lectura que su niño hace en la casa al coleccionar textos y libros de no ficción que sean de interés para su niño. También puede hablar con su niño acerca de lo que aprende al leer solo y al escuchar la lectura en voz alta del género de no ficción.

Es de gran ayuda, si antes de leerle textos de no ficción a su niño le hace preguntas como:

- ¿Qué sabes acerca de (los murciélagos)?

- ¿Qué preguntas tienes acerca de (los murciélagos)?

Considere parar la lectura en voz alta para preguntarle a su niño que está aprendiendo y si aún tiene alguna duda.

Después de haber leído hágale a su niño preguntas como:

- ¿En este libro qué aprendiste acerca de (los murciélagos)?

- ¿Qué aprendiste que te sorprendió?

- ¿Qué preguntas tienes todavía acerca de (los murciélagos)?

Espero que continúen disfrutando de la lectura que comparten juntos. ¡Feliz lectura!

Sinceramente,

 Dear Parent or Guardian,

Our class just finished the eighth unit of the *Making Meaning*® program. In this unit, the students explored important ideas in fiction and nonfiction. They identified what they felt were the important ideas in books and stories and supported their opinions with evidence from the text. *Determining important ideas* is a powerful strategy for helping readers understand and communicate what they read. The students also continued to visualize and make inferences to help them understand and enjoy stories. Socially, the students developed the group skills of giving reasons for their ideas and asking clarifying questions.

You can support your child's reading life at home. While reading aloud to your child, consider stopping to discuss questions such as:

- What is something interesting you learned in the part I just read?

- What is most important to understand or remember in the part I just read? Why do you think it's important?

- What did you picture in your mind when you heard that part?

After reading nonfiction books, you can help your child think more deeply about the books by asking questions such as:

- What are some important ideas you remember from the reading?

- Why do you think those are some of the important ideas from the story?

I hope you and your child enjoy your reading conversations!

Sincerely,

Apreciado padre de familia o guardián:

Nuestra clase acaba de finalizar la octava unidad del programa "*Making Meaning.*®" Durante esta unidad los estudiantes exploraron ideas importantes en los géneros de ficción y no ficción. Ellos identificaron cuales creían que eran las ideas importantes de las historias y los libros. Y así mismo apoyaron sus opiniones con muestras del texto. *El determinar ideas importantes* es una estrategia muy poderosa que ayuda al lector a entender y comunicar lo que leyó. Los estudiantes continuaron visualizando y haciendo deducciones para entender y disfrutar las historias. Socialmente, los estudiantes desarrollaron destrezas de grupo al poder dar razones del porqué tuvieron una idea y al poder hacer preguntas para clarificar.

Mientras le lee en voz alta a su niño, considere parar para hablar acerca de preguntas como:

- ¿Qué es algo interesante que aprendiste en la parte que te acabo de leer?

- ¿Qué es lo más importante de entender o recordar en la parte que te acabo de leer? ¿Por qué crees que es importante?

- ¿Qué imagen te vino a la mente cuando escuchaste esa parte?

Después de leer libros de no ficción, usted le puede ayudar a su niño a pensar más a fondo acerca de los libros al hacer preguntas como:

- ¿Cuáles son algunas de las ideas importantes que recuerdas de la lectura?

- ¿Por qué crees que esas son las ideas importantes de la historia?

¡Espero que usted y su niño disfruten de sus conversaciones acerca de la lectura!

Sinceramente,

 Dear Parent or Guardian,

We have come to the end of our school year and the end of the *Making Meaning*® grade 3 reading comprehension program. The children have shown great enthusiasm for the variety of texts we read aloud and the conversations we had about reading. They eagerly explored a number of reading comprehension strategies, including: visualizing, questioning, exploring text features, making inferences and determining important ideas. The use of these comprehension strategies strengthened the children's reading comprehension skills and should continue to be a source of support for them for years to come.

In the last unit of the *Making Meaning* program, the students made summer reading recommendations to their classmates. They reflected on their growth as readers and as members of a reading community and continued to develop the group skills of giving reasons for their opinions and discussing their opinions respectfully.

Summer is a great time for trips to the library and quiet moments curled up with a good book. Your child made a list of books he or she would like to read this summer. Please help your child find the books on the list and encourage him or her to read the books and discuss them with friends. Of course, your child might want to add new books to the list as the summer progresses. Every so often, you might want to read some of the books aloud to your child and discuss their meaning together. Throughout the summer, encourage reading for enjoyment.

Thank you for helping to make the home-school connection successful. Your participation was essential. I hope along the way you and your child enjoyed the reading and the conversations about books.

Have a great summer!

Sincerely,

Apreciado padre de familia o guardián:

Hemos llegado al final del año escolar y al final del programa de comprensión de lectura para el tercer grado de "*Making Meaning.®*" Los niños han mostrado mucho entusiasmo por la variedad de textos que leímos en voz alta y por las conversaciones que tuvimos acerca de lectura. Ellos exploraron afanosamente un número de estrategias de comprensión de lectura, incluyendo: visualizar, el hacer preguntas, el explorar los aspectos del texto, el hacer deducciones, determinar ideas importantes, y el analizar la estructura de un texto. El uso de estas estrategias de comprensión fortalecen las destrezas de comprensión de lectura que los niños tienen y continuará siendo una fuente de apoyo para ellos por muchos años más.

En la última unidad del programa "*Making Meaning*", los estudiantes hicieron recomendaciones de lectura a sus compañeros. Ellos también se pusieron a reflexionar sobre el desarrollo que han tenido como lectores y como miembros de la comunidad de lectores y continuaron las destrezas de grupo al dar las razones por sus opiniones y al discutir estas opiniones en una manera respetuosa.

El verano es un gran momento para hacer viajes a la biblioteca y para pasar ratos sentados en silencio con un buen libro. Su niño hizo una lista de los libros que le gustaría leer este verano. Por favor ayúdelo a encontrar los libros que tiene en la lista y aliéntelo a que los lea y a que hable acerca de ellos con sus amigos. Es posible que a medida que progrese el verano su niño quiera añadir otros libros a la lista. De vez en cuando, tal vez usted quiera leerle en voz alta algunos de los libros a su niño y hablar acerca del significado. Durante el verano, aliente a su niño a que lea para divertirse.

Le agradezco su ayuda en hacer que la conexión de la casa con la escuela fuera un éxito. Su participación fue esencial. Espero que durante el proceso usted y su niño hayan disfrutado de la lectura y las conversaciones acerca de los libros.

¡Espero que tengan un buen verano!

Sinceramente,

Contents
from *Reptiles* by Melissa Stewart

Contents

Making Meaning® Reorder Information
SECOND EDITION

Kindergarten

Complete Classroom Package MM2-CPK

Contents: Teacher's Manual, Orientation Handbook and DVDs, and 27 trade books

Available separately:

Classroom materials without trade books	MM2-TPK
Teacher's Manual	MM2-TMK
Trade book set (27 books)	MM2-TBSK

Grade 1

Complete Classroom Package MM2-CP1

Contents: Teacher's Manual, Orientation Handbook and DVDs, Assessment Resource Book, and 28 trade books

Available separately:

Classroom materials without trade books	MM2-TP1
Teacher's Manual	MM2-TM1
Assessment Resource Book	MM2-AB1
Trade book set (28 books)	MM2-TBS1

Grade 2

Complete Classroom Package MM2-CP2

Contents: Teacher's Manual, Orientation Handbook and DVDs, class set (25 Student Response Books, Assessment Resource Book), and 29 trade books

Available separately:

Classroom materials without trade books	MM2-TP2
Teacher's Manual	MM2-TM2
Replacement class set	MM2-RCS2
CD-ROM Grade 2 Reproducible Materials	MM2-CDR2
Trade book set (29 books)	MM2-TBS2

Grade 3

Complete Classroom Package MM2-CP3

Contents: Teacher's Manual (2 volumes), Orientation Handbook and DVDs, class set (25 Student Response Books, Assessment Resource Book), and 26 trade books

Available separately:

Classroom materials without trade books	MM2-TP3
Teacher's Manual, vol. 1	MM2-TM3-V1
Teacher's Manual, vol. 2	MM2-TM3-V2
Replacement class set	MM2-RCS3
CD-ROM Grade 3 Reproducible Materials	MM2-CDR3
Trade book set (26 books)	MM2-TBS3

Grade 4

Complete Classroom Package MM2-CP4

Contents: Teacher's Manual (2 volumes), Orientation Handbook and DVDs, class set (30 Student Response Books, Assessment Resource Book), and 24 trade books

Available separately:

Classroom materials without trade books	MM2-TP4
Teacher's Manual, vol. 1	MM2-TM4-V1
Teacher's Manual, vol. 2	MM2-TM4-V2
Replacement class set	MM2-RCS4
CD-ROM Grade 4 Reproducible Materials	MM2-CDR4
Trade book set (24 books)	MM2-TBS4

Grade 5

Complete Classroom Package MM2-CP5

Contents: Teacher's Manual (2 volumes), Orientation Handbook and DVDs, class set (30 Student Response Books, Assessment Resource Book), and 19 trade books

Available separately:

Classroom materials without trade books	MM2-TP5
Teacher's Manual, vol. 1	MM2-TM5-V1
Teacher's Manual, vol. 2	MM2-TM5-V2
Replacement class set	MM2-RCS5
CD-ROM Grade 5 Reproducible Materials	MM2-CDR5
Trade book set (19 books)	MM2-TBS5

Grade 6

Complete Classroom Package MM2-CP6

Contents: Teacher's Manual (2 volumes), Orientation Handbook and DVDs, class set (30 Student Response Books, Assessment Resource Book), and 18 trade books

Available separately:

Classroom materials without trade books	MM2-TP6
Teacher's Manual, vol. 1	MM2-TM6-V1
Teacher's Manual, vol. 2	MM2-TM6-V2
Replacement class set	MM2-RCS5
CD-ROM Grade 6 Reproducible Materials	MM2-CDR6
Trade book set (18 books)	MM2-TBS6

Ordering Information:

To order call 800.666.7270 * fax 510.842.0348
log on to devstu.org * e-mail pubs@devstu.org

Or Mail Your Order to:

Developmental Studies Center * Publications Department
2000 Embarcadero, Suite 305 * Oakland, CA 94606-5300

DEVELOPMENTAL
STUDIES CENTER™